WINSTON R. HEWITT

THROUGH THOSE LIVING PILLARS

MAN AND NATURE IN THE WORKS OF EMILE ZOLA

DE PROPRIETATIBUS LITTERARUM

edenda curat
C. H. VAN SCHOONEVELD
Indiana University

Series Practica, 75

THROUGH THOSE LIVING PILLARS

Man and Nature
in the Works of Emile Zola

by

WINSTON HEWITT

California State College
Dominguez Hills

1974
MOUTON
THE HAGUE · PARIS

LIBRARY OF CONGRESS CATALOG CARD NUMBER: 73-85971

Printed in The Netherlands by Mouton & Co., The Hague

La Nature est un temple où de vivants piliers
Laissent parfois sortir de confuses paroles ;
L'homme y passe à travers des forêts de symboles
Qui l'observent avec des regards familiers.

Baudelaire

ACKNOWLEDGMENTS

I wish to express my gratitude to my friends and colleagues Professors Yvone Lenard and Ephriam Sando for their valuable editorial suggestions.

W. R. H.

PREFACE

Partout la nature s'éveille.

Hugo.

Nature permeates the prose of Emile Zola from the earliest short story to the conclusion of his last novel. The phenomena of the natural world play varying roles in the novels and provide the setting for most of the short stories. Nature is virtually omnipresent in such novels as *La Faute de l'abbé Mouret* and *La Terre*. In his outline for the latter, the author stresses the predominant role that the earth is to play: "C'est l'héroïne de mon livre.... Un personnage énorme toujours présent, emplissant le livre." (531)[1] The only novel which excludes, for all practical purposes, the presence of nature is *Pot-Bouille;* the exceptions being some rare references to drizzling rain and the mention of a pale, cold moon that illumines the lurid scene of a woman who secretly bears her own child before abandoning it. (410-411) The vitality of nature would have otherwise lifted and refreshed the intentionally putrescent atmosphere of this novel.

In general, great significance is accorded to nature in Zola's novels and in most of his short stories. The main body of this monograph will be devoted to ascertaining the roles and the importance that Zola assigns to

---

[1] The letters *DL* for *Documents littéraires*, *MH* for *Mes Haines*, *RE* for *Le Roman expérimental*, *RN* for *Les Romanciers naturalistes*, and *UC* for *Une Campagne* designate the critical works which provide the primary source materials for the Introduction, but are not named in context. The letter *C* designates *Correspondance*, and *M*, *Mélanges*. All novels are named in context. Therefore, each quotation from a novel is followed only by the page number(s) placed within parentheses. *LFAM*, an exception, designates *La Faute de l'abbé Mouret* when we quote from an earlier short work, "Le Printemps — journal d'un convalescent", found in the appendix to this novel. When a short story is referred to, the volume is designated by the letters *CN* for both the *Contes à Ninon* and *Nouveaux Contes à Ninon*, and *CN I* and *CN II* for the first and second volumes of *Contes et Nouvelles*. All quotations are from the Bernouard edition of the *Œuvres complètes* edited by Maurice Le Blond (50 vols., Paris, 1927-29).

nature in his works, particularly up to 1893, the year that marks the completion of the *Rougon-Macquart* series, and — for most critics — the waning of his power as a novelist. Moreover, from this juncture until his death in 1902, the relations of man and nature clearly undergo considerable modification. Some of the changes in emphasis that the later Zola places on both man and nature will be examined in the final chapter.

Essentially, in the work of Zola, our attention is drawn to how man returns to nature, how nature purifies and pacifies him, how it releases man's preconscious and unconscious desires and bares his anxieties, how nature participates as an active accomplice of love, how nature reflects man's feelings and emotions, and varyingly reveals either a hostile or benevolent aspect. The above is in fact a summary of the main body of the present work. It is preceded by an introductory chapter containing Zola's doctrinaire views of the role of nature in the study of man.[2] There is, as well, a concluding chapter on the novelist's particular vision of nature and how this insight and nature itself extend man's psyche.

Zola's literary sources of inspiration for the thematic examples and their specific images, expression, and syntax, are so overwhelmingly rich throughout the entire nineteenth century in French literature that they have been virtually excluded from this study, but may constitute the basis of a future work. Even relatively comprehensive footnotes would have engulfed the present text, while a sampling in so broad a field would have frustrated the scholars in their specific fields. However, as a poetic compromise, echoes of these sources will appear at the head of all chapters and sections in the form of epigraphs selected from the works of only four French romantic poets.

Many of the longer quotations and resumés of action and their setting may seem lengthy reminders, unnecessary for the Zola scholar. Those are intended for the general reader of French literature who has not read extensively in Zola's works.

> Mon verre n'est pas grand, mais je bois dans mon verre.
>
> Musset

This study was originally undertaken as a doctoral dissertation, completed in May 1963, and microfilmed by University Microfilms, Inc., Ann Arbor,

---

[2] For a systematic study of the development of the role of nature in French literature through romanticism, see Gustave Charlier, *Le Sentiment de la nature chez les romantiques français (1760-1830)* (Paris: Fontemoing, 1912).

Michigan. The present monograph represents a completely revised version, reduced in documented examples, and expanded in other aspects, of that original dissertation. The dissertation has been available to scholars in the field since 1963, and use has been made of it in publication elsewhere without any acknowledgment, not even bibliographical inclusion.[3] Zola specialists are likely to recognize in this present volume not only similarities in some concepts and themes (which in essence are readily discernible by many), but even parallels in the wording of various passages from the dissertation as having appeared in print elsewhere, unacknowledged. Rather therefore than any reader believing that this study has borrowed without acknowledgment from other sources, it must be pointed out at the outset that the reverse is true. But, then, in the scholarly world, all are concerned with the advancement of knowledge, and each researcher builds *in his own way* upon the works of his predecessors.

---

[3] Such bibliographical inclusion would obviously have rendered this paragraph unnecessary.

TABLE OF CONTENTS

14 TABLE OF CONTENTS

I

INTRODUCTION: A VIEW OF NATURE

La nature, sans doute, est comme on veut la prendre.

Musset

Zola the critic explains Zola the novelist. The novelist, one may also observe, explains the critic. An overview of Zola's criticism of the presence and role of nature in the study of man as revealed by his forays into French literary analysis will elucidate the great importance he places on nature in his prose works. "Nous avons fait à la nature, au vaste monde, une place tout aussi large qu'à l'homme. Nous n'admettons pas que l'homme seul existe et que seul il importe, persuadés au contraire qu'il est un simple résultat, et que, pour avoir le drame humain réel et complet, il faut demander à tout ce qui est." (RE 186)

Nature, or the natural world and its phenomena, falls easily and intrinsically into definitions of naturalism. Zola writes that he did not invent the word, that Montaigne had already used it with its modern meaning. (UC 105) Zola defines naturalism in literature as "le retour à la nature et à l'homme, l'observation directe, l'anatomie exacte, l'acceptation de la peinture de ce qui est" (RE 95), or more succinctly as "une enquête sur la nature, les êtres et les choses" (RE 102). This appeal for a purely objective investigation of man and his total environment would confirm a prevalent tendency on the part of some critics, especially René Dumesnil,[1] to classify the naturalists as the second generation of the realists. Whether Zola himself probes as scientifically with his literary scalpel into nature as in man, that is, whether he observes both with equally incisive objectivity, a capital criterion for naturalism, will be examined in a concluding chapter, "The Screen".

Nature, according to Zola, was largely absent from the literary works of the seventeenth century; in the novels, "la nature n'a aucun rôle à

[1] René Dumesnil, *Le Réalisme et le naturalisme* (Paris: Del Duca de Gigord, 1955), pp. 319-406.

jouer" (RE 185). Nature, which had not yet been "humanized", was considered "inferior and indifferent" (CN I 59). Seldom did it provide more than the décor for a castle. The intellectually abstracted characters of seventeenth-century literature were not only unaware of nature, but physical surroundings in general. Zola charges that the writers of that period were themselves insensitive to nature, that even La Fontaine does not indicate any positive enjoyment of nature *per se:* "A peine La Fontaine osait-il s'égarer dans les champs humides de rosée."[2] Judging by the poet's own works,[3] and according to other critics,[4] this seems an erroneous premise. However, in an essay about the Parisian suburbs, Zola judges the fabulist less severely: "La Fontaine lui-même, le poète qui, de son temps, a le plus senti la nature n'a pas un vers pour la banlieue parisienne; on en trouve bien chez lui le lointain parfum, mais il n'y faut point chercher la moindre note exacte et précise." (CN I 59) As far as Zola is generally concerned, the seventeenth century simply remained aloof to nature: "L'art antique avait divinisé la nature, l'art moderne l'a humanisée, tandis que notre art classique la passait tout simplement sous silence." (CN I 59-60)

For Zola, nature makes its debut only in some philosophical and idyllic works of the eighteenth century. At that time men of letters began to reevaluate man in relation to his physical surroundings: "... les arbres, les eaux, les montagnes, les grands bois deviennent des êtres, reprennent leur place dans le mécanisme du monde; l'homme n'est plus une abstraction intellectuelle, la nature le détermine et le complète." (RE 95) Jean-Jacques Rousseau and Denis Diderot reacted against classicism for its abstraction of man, its isolation of man's intellect from both his body and environment.

These two literary figures sired the opposing schools of nineteenth-century literature. In contradistinction to the pantheistic, lyrical, and philosophical Rousseau, the romantics' father, stands Diderot, the 'positivist', the naturalists' ancestor. Zola has a tendency to construct literary genealogies, not to mention the family tree for his *Rougon-*

---

[2] F. W. J. Hemmings and R. J. Niess, eds., *Émile Zola: Salons* (Paris: Minard, 1959), p. 133.

[3] See, for example, the fable "Le Songe d'un habitant du Mogol", where the character seeks out solitude in a discreet nature, in Jean de la Fontaine, *Fables, Contes et Nouvelles*, ed. Bibliothèque de la Pléiade (1954), pp. 267-268.

[4] For example, Antoine Adam, *Histoire de la littérature française au XVIIe siècle*, Vol. IV (Paris: Domat, 1954), p. 12, writes that La Fontaine "aimait extrêmement les jardins, les fleurs, les ombrages, toute une vie calme et belle, étrangère aux vaines agitations des hommes".

Macquart series. Among the progeny of Rousseau whom Zola examines, relevant to the study of man's relationship with nature, are François-René de Chateaubriand, Victor Hugo, George Sand and Théophile Gautier. Zola, on the other hand, considers Stendhal, Honoré de Balzac, Gustave Flaubert, Edmond and Jules de Goncourt, and finally his fellow naturalists and himself to be in direct descent from Diderot.

Zola attributes to Rousseau the rediscovery of nature in literature: "Il fallait que Rousseau vînt pour qu'un attendrissement universel se déclarât, et pour qu'on se mît à embrasser les chênes comme des frères. Aujourd'hui, notre passion des champs nous vient de ce grand mouvement naturaliste du XVIIIe siècle." (CN I 59) With Rousseau, nature assumes a significant role in the study of the total man, but the subsequent romantic writers exploit nature primarily in order to reinforce and to enhance the expression of their personal sentiments and emotions. "Rousseau a le premier pleuré devant la nature; mais il raisonnait encore, tandis que ses fils n'ont plus trouvé que des larmes." (DL 25) Romantic lyricism depicts nature as overly dramatic and grandiose. After Rousseau initiated nature into literature, the romantics spiritualized it, and, "avec Chateaubriand, Lamartine, Victor Hugo, on entra dans un panthéisme poétique, où sanglotait la fraternité des êtres et des choses" (CN I 59). Zola, too, entered there at times, perhaps best exemplified in the second of the three books of *La Faute de l'abbé Mouret* and in the short story "Simplice".

Chateaubriand, whom the critic associates with the expansive and infinite aspects of nature, brought back from America "a sentiment of broad horizons" (DL 17). Chateaubriand creates in his René the French prototype of the tormented poet who feels a fraternal affinity with nature so tender that it elicits tears and a strong wish for absorption of self into the panoramic scene stretching out before him (DL 26). The mergence with nature ultimately takes curious form for René's creator. On his deathbed Chateaubriand requested that his tombstone, unmarked, be placed at the top of the Grand-Bé reef that overlooks the sea. For Zola, he becomes transubstantiated into this gigantic reef "qui défie les tempêtes, qui reste éternellement noir et vainqueur dans les orages" (DL 10). And twenty-seven years after Chateaubriand's death, the town of Saint-Malo commemorated his memory with official speeches during the day and fireworks in the evening; man's festivities ceded to the calm and peace of night. "Oui, cela a dû être bon pour l'écueil et pour le grand mort, qui dédaigneux de l'hommage des hommes, n'a voulu que l'éternelle acclamation de l'Océan à ses pieds." (DL 15)

Victor Hugo, personally less involved with nature, distorts it out of all proportion. "Un jardinet bourgeois devient un Eden.... Les roses sont grosses comme des choux." (DL 68) This comment from Zola's mocking explication of Hugo's "Petit Paul" provides us one of the more striking instances of Zola's critical judgment reversed by his actual practice. In *La Faute de l'abbé Mouret*, the park named the Paradou, a Provençal rendering of "Paradise", literally 'becomes an Eden', too. Although this Garden of Eden for Serge and Albine was never qualified as small, nevertheless the reader gains the impression that its vastness expands more and more, almost infinitely, from chapter to chapter. Furthermore, its flowers and other plant life, untended for the past century, have grown enormously in size. Perhaps its roses have not attained the magnitude of cabbages, but its legendary tree certainly possesses both mythic proportions and qualities.[5] The Eden transfiguration also figures into the criticism directed against Hugo's *Les Chansons des rues et des bois*, doubling the ironic contradiction between Zola the critic and Zola the novelist: "Vous ou moi, nous serions sortis à pied, nous aurions chanté les bois tels qu'ils sont, sans les transfigurer en Edens, sans les voir en pleine lumière idéale." (MH 83)

Whereas Hugo's distorted imagination propels him too far from the reality of the modern world viewed by Zola, the idealized misrepresentations of nature in the works of George Sand pose potentially dangerous implications for her readers. As Zola proceeds to construct the French romantic family tree, he makes the following observation about George Sand: "... cette fille attendrie et rêveuse de Rousseau, qui a l'adoration passionnée de la nature, mais qui ne la voit jamais, comme son père, qu'à travers les imaginations les plus chimériques." (UC 103) This extreme fancifulness of her inventive imagination corroded her literary genius. Yet she developed a deep and abiding love for nature during her childhood as she played in the woods around the Château de Nohant, her family seat. Zola also relates that when she was first placed in a convent in Paris at the age of thirteen, she wept, yearning for the rustic nature from which she had been severed. Her subsequent joyful consolation upon discovering the vast garden there may have a literary echo in Zola's *Le Voeu d'une morte*, in the heroine's childhood memories of dashing exuberantly about the trees in the playground of the convent (95).

In George Sand's *Indiana*, Zola seems particularly drawn to Sir Ralph's

---

[5] Moreover, F. W. J. Hemmings in "The Secret Sources of *La Faute de l'abbé Mouret*", *French Studies*, XIII (1959), pp. 227-228, points out Zola's literary debt to Hugo here, for a garden in Hugo's *Les Misérables* no doubt served as the primary model for Zola's larger Paradou.

quest through a wild, virginal nature of a suitably picturesque site for committing suicide. In Sand's *Mauprat*, the rustic philosopher Patience represents for Zola "la nature, la santé des campagnes, l'homme nouveau poussant aux champs comme un chêne vigoureux" (DL 177). Such a man of nature has literary siblings among some of Zola's characters whom we shall examine in a later chapter. Moreover, Zola finds charm and beauty in the nature that impregnates this novel, particularly in those scenes in which a nightingale accompanies the lovers' conversations with its song.[6] He agrees that readers nurtured in the romantic tradition should not necessarily be deprived of the charming atmosphere that pervades such fairy tales. But, on the other hand, he holds Sand responsible for creating "toute une génération de rêveuses et de raisonneuses insupportables" (DL 318). Immersed in the idealized fabrications of her dream world, they are unable to cope with the realities of everyday situations. The backgrounds of her love scenes are false and illusory: "Ce ne sont que tourelles éclairées par la lune, que promenades sous les allées au chant du rossignol, que longs serments et que baisers assurant une éternité de jouissance." (DL 318) Curiously enough, this accusation of romantic sentimentality could be directed to the critic himself, particularly in *Le Rêve* where similar images and scenes prevail in profusion. Zola contends that through sustained exposure to George Sand's lyrical idealizations, the reader could drift easily away from our real world and slip subsequently into "a cerebral breakdown and sensual perversion". The naturalistic novel must bare life as it is lived on this earth; Zola affirms that "la vertu et le bonheur sont ... dans l'acceptation du vrai, dans le juste équilibre de l'homme avec la nature qui l'entoure" (DL 318).

Zola blames the poets of the generation of 1830 for further alienation of man from both nature and other men. Nature, as they paint it, sheds no direct light upon the study of man, but hangs instead as a meaningless backdrop behind their dreams and nightmares. The critic asserts that despite their revelation of new horizons in the world of nature, the romantic man is even less real and human than the stiff and abstract classic one (RE 60). Zola reproaches Théophile Gautier for employing description only for its own sake as well as for art. Nature provides no determining environment for man, but exists by and for itself, removed from him. Devoid of human movement, Gautier's landscapes represent "un retour à la nature morte des didactiques" (DL 114). From the "silence sépulcral"

---

[6] The nightingale's song also punctuates the phases of Henri and Henriette's love in Guy de Maupassant's "Une Partie de campagne", *Œuvres complètes de Guy de Maupassant*, Vol. XIII (Paris: Conard, 1908), pp. 108-113.

of his works, "aucun frisson humain ne monte de cette terre morte" (RE 187).

In general, Zola finds that the romantics continue to abstract man by creating character types, while the naturalists replace the eighteenth-century metaphysical being with the physiological man integrated in a deterministic milieu. However, Zola reluctantly associates Stendhal with the latter group, primarily because this author allegedly does not allow nature to intervene and act upon the characters in his novels. Zola judges Stendhal's studies of man to be incomplete, concentrating solely on the psychological aspect of man to the almost total exclusion of the physiological and the environmental aspects (RN 73-74). The brain of the Stendhalian character functions in isolation from the other body organs. The mirror that Stendhal professes to have taken along a road "ne réfléchit que la tête de l'homme, la partie noble, sans nous donner le corps ni les lieux environnants" (RN 80). He thereby perpetrates the classical procedure of abstracting the soul, "sans vouloir rechercher l'action que les rouages de la machine humaine et que la nature tout entière exercent évidemment sur elle" (RN 74).

The critic flatly refuses the concept of a bodiless exalted mind operating independently in a void, and free of those senses that normally communicate stimuli from the outer world to hasten or retard psychological movements (RN 77). As supporting evidence of his allegation that Stendhal is preoccupied exclusively with the psyche, Zola refers us to the famous scene of Julien Sorel taking the hand of Mme de Rênal into his own as she sits beside him and chats with Mme Derville, in *Le Rouge et le Noir*. It is evening, and the three are seated under the branches of a linden-tree in the garden. Zola writes that the physical surroundings play no part in this little drama, that its action could have been performed absolutely anywhere at all with the single provision that it take place in darkness. He concedes that Julien's inner tension over executing the valorous duty he has assigned himself might make him insensitive to the outer surroundings, but that Mme de Rênal should remain so, too, Zola deems inexcusable. "Donnez l'épisode à un écrivain pour qui les milieux existent, et dans la défaite de cette femme, il fera entrer la nuit, avec ses odeurs, avec ses voix, avec ses voluptés molles." (RN 78) Contrary to Zola's assertion that nature plays no role whatsoever in this particular scene, Stendhal, who earlier mentioned the hot wind and large clouds of an approaching storm, does indeed record at least the awakening of the emotionally aroused woman's auditory sense to the sounds in nature: "Elle écoutait avec délices les gémissements du vent dans l'épais feuillage du tilleul, et le bruit de quelques gouttes rares qui commençaient à tomber sur ses feuilles les plus basses.''[7]

Yet, Zola designates Stendhal as the literary link that joins the eighteenth-century to the contemporary novel in that he is the first novelist to demonstrate the influence of geographical surroundings upon the characters. Stendhal's law of milieus, condensed in the prefatory statement to *La Chartreuse de Parme*, states that each advance of two hundred leagues northward furnishes a new landscape and a new novel. And, consequently, the characters' personalities differ, too. As an example, Zola refers to Mlle de la Môle and the Duchesse Sanseverina from two of Stendhal's novels. The dissimilarity of the climates of the countries in which they live and of the societies that they frequent explain in large part why each expresses her love differently (RN 98).

But Zola holds a reservation for *Parme*. Although its Italians are "réels, et non des Français déguisés", nature is totally absent: "...jamais le paysage, le climat, l'heure de la journée, le temps qu'il fait, la nature en un mot n'interviendra et n'agira sur les personnages. ...il met l'être humain dans la nature et déclare ensuite que l'âme seule étant noble, l'âme seule a droit de cité en littérature." (RN 76) However, Zola is overly harsh with his absolute negations. It is true that nature rarely appears here, but also that its beauty, calmness, and solitude do on occasion affect the hero. The infatuated Fabrice, summoned by his mother, reluctantly goes to Belgirate on Lake Maggiore. The mountain air and the majesty and calmness of the lake pacify him, changing "en douce mélancolie le chagrin de Fabrice, voisin de la colère".[8] At midnight a few days later, his travels bring him to the shores of Lake Como. A "profound tranquility" reigns over the lake waters and in the starry sky "veiled by a light mist".[9] "...l'âme de Fabrice ne put résister à cette beauté sublime."[10] As he sits on a rock jutting out into the lake, his reactions parallel, at least briefly, those of many romantic heroes, not to mention many of Zola's characters: "... l'aspect seul de la beauté sublime le portait à l'attendrissement, et ôtait à ses chagrins leur pointe âpre et dure. ... de douces larmes mouillèrent ses yeux, et il trouva, à peu de frais, les moments les plus heureux qu'il eût goûtés depuis longtemps."[11] And, on the evening Fabrice

---

[7] Stendhal, *Le Rouge et le Noir*, in *Romans et nouvelles de Stendhal*, ed. Bibliothèque de la Pléiade, Vol. I (1966), p. 268.

[8] Stendhal, *La Chartreuse de Parme*, in *Romans et nouvelles de Stendhal*, ed. Bibliothèque de la Pléiade, Vol. II (1964), p. 164.

[9] *La Chartreuse de Parme*, p. 165.

[10] P. 166.

[11] P. 166.

enters prison, the "sublime spectacle" of the majestic beauty of the Alpine setting "moves" him.[12] Before he goes to bed in his cell that night, he scans the stars and the immense chain of snow-covered mountains. "Je conçois que Clélia Conti se plaise dans cette solitude aérienne; on est ici à mille lieues au-dessus des petitesses et des méchancetés qui nous occupent là-bas."[13]

In spite of Stendhal's preoccupation with man's psyche, but because his studies of it were exhaustive, Zola names him as one of naturalism's teachers. He only wonders whether the continuous, relentless probing into the regions of the brain caused Stendhal's characters to suffer from migraine headaches. On behalf of these suffering souls, Zola directs the following plea to their creator-tormenter: "Par grâce, laissez-les donc un peu tranquilles; laissez-les quelquefois vivre de la bonne vie des bêtes, simplement, dans la poussée de l'instinct, au milieu de la saine nature." (RN 85).

In contrast to Stendhal, who delved unmercifully into every mental and psychological movement of his characters, "Balzac a pris l'homme tout entier, avec ses organes, avec les milieux naturels et sociaux, et il a complété les expériences du psychologue par celles du physiologiste." (RN 104) In going beyond the realm of the mind, Balzac's studies of man relate him to his immediate environment. Balzac observes him as "une plante tenant au sol" (RN 75). As opposed to the Stendhalian character, "une machine intellectuelle et passionnelle parfaitement montée", stands Balzac's, "un homme en chair et en os, avec son vêtement et l'air qui l'enveloppe" (RN 77). Zola expresses his strong preference for the being who lives to the one who only reasons. Claiming Balzac as the first literary figure to demonstrate in each novel the direct influence of the environment upon the formation of the characters, Zola recognizes him as "notre véritable père" (RN 64).

After "the descriptive orgies of romanticism" (RE 185) that ushered in the nineteenth century, Zola sees description settling down to its exacting scientific role with Balzac, Flaubert, and other realists. He recommends Flaubert as a model writer for maintaining a proper balance of environmental description to the characters (RE 188). Never excessive, it never submerges them. Flaubert reserves description, marked by sobriety of line and color, for the explanation of man and his actions (RN 115). He authenticates the description of each physical setting, either by visiting the actual locale or by seeking a likely facsimile for an imagined one (RN 112).

[12] P. 310.
[13] P. 312-313.

In examining Flaubert's *Salammbô*, Zola is especially drawn to the first chapter, an opening chapter that excels all others in French literature (RN 188). The moonlit scene of Salammbô invoking the goddess Tanit during the festivities in the gardens of Hamilcar particularly intrigues Zola. It is natural to expect Zola to single out garden settings since they figure importantly in a vast number of his own works. And it is in a moonlit garden setting that Angélique of *Le Rêve* invokes and virtually brings into being her Prince Charming. Zola's interest in Flaubert's *La Tentation de saint Antoine* lies primarily in the last chapter. He gives a résumé and even quotes a passage that depicts the saint's descent from the infinitely great to the infinitesimally small, from animal life through vegetative growth, and finally down into mineral inanimateness. The desire to lose one's identity in nature haunts a number of Zola's characters, too. Differing unconscious motives that fragment this general theme will compel us to examine its variations hereafter at much greater length.

Edmond and Jules de Goncourt are other literary fathers acknowledged by the naturalists. Zola praises the intense personal life suffusing their descriptions of nature. Each object, while preserving its objective essence, is reborn through the vibrations of the Goncourts' conjoined hypersensitive nervous system. "On dirait la nature ... animée, exaltée, les cailloux ayant des sentiments d'êtres vivants, les personnages donnant de leur tristesse ou de leur joie aux horizons. L'œuvre entière devenait une sorte de vaste névrose." (RN 187-188) The critic, as might be expected, sanctions their animation of a nature invested with human emotions and sensations, since he employs this poetic device of pathetic fallacy so profusely and extensively throughout his own works. "L'homme apparaît, se mêle aux choses, les anime par la vibration nerveuse de son émotion. Tout le génie des Goncourt est dans cette traduction si vivante de la nature, dans ces frissons notés, ces chuchotements balbutiés, ces mille souffles rendus sensibles." (RE 188) Isolated, this last quotation seems equally applicable to some romantic writers — Chateaubriand and Lamartine, to name but two.

Zola praises the total integration of the Goncourts' characters with their surroundings. "L'art nouveau est là: on n'étudie plus les hommes comme de simples curiosités intellectuelles, dégagées de la nature ambiante; on croit au contraire que les hommes n'existent pas seuls, qu'ils tiennent aux paysages, que les paysages dans lesquels ils marchent les complètent et les expliquent." (RN 188-189) For example, in *Madame Gervaisais*, Zola extols how nature both reacts on the heroine and reflects her sentimental and mental states of being. "Dès lors, les paysages de-

viennent une nécessité. Ils arrivent, chacun à son heure, pour aider, com-
battre, modifier, déterminer un état d'âme.... La nature se mêle intime-
ment à l'humanité, elle en est ainsi le cadre ingénieux et nécessaire."
(MH 299)

The Goncourts' characters and settings, so redolent with nuances,
spring vividly to life in the mind of the reader. Nothing is left to his
imagination; he no longer needs to create his own décor for the action.
Zola claims that those readers who complain about excessive length of
descriptive passages (an accusation often leveled at Zola himself) and about
personal expression coloring reality possess dulled senses and lack poetic
sensitivity. "Est-ce que la nuit a cette douceur mélancolique? est-ce que
les berges d'une rivière déroulent des coins d'ombre si adorable? Ce sont
des aveugles qui nient les couleurs." (RN 189) For Zola, the Goncourts'
style is the most personal he has encountered; and, yet, "la phrase a la
couleur du ciel dont elle parle, l'odeur de la fleur qu'elle nomme!" (RN
190) Their *Germinie Lacerteux* proves them to be the first novelists to
carefully study the inhabitants of Paris in their physical surroundings, as
well as the first to paint "les paysages désolés de la banlieue" (RE 101).
Zola's own works exhibit an abiding interest in these subjects. Zola never
fails to acknowledge the great debt he and the naturalistic movement owe
the Goncourts.

Like the Goncourt brothers, Emile Erckmann and Alexandre Chatrian
co-authored a number of works. Their prose and dramatic efforts appeared
under the signature of Erckmann-Chatrian. For Zola, their characters were
puppets that lacked life, but their countrysides possessed it: "Dans nos
théâtres, ce sont les campagnes qui sont de carton et de bois; ici, ce sont
les personnages. Les champs vivent, pleurent et sourient; le soleil luit
largement, et la grande nature s'étale avec puissance, admirablement ré-
sumée en quelques traits justes et forts.... Imaginez des automates se
promenant au milieu de la création de Dieu." (MH 144)

Although the surroundings apparently neither influenced nor infused
life in Erckmann-Chatrian's characters, Zola finds other instances where
they do affect man. For example, he points out that the geographical
milieu strongly determines any writer. Furthermore, he contends that the
reader, too, will derive an even greater appreciation of an author's works
if he can situate the writer in his formative environment. The natural
surroundings greatly influence the intellectual and spiritual formation of
an author. In striking illustration, Zola contrasts the writers Ernest
Renan and Claude Bernard, each of whom was brought up by a priest.
The critic explains that Renan's childhood spent on the fog-steeped coast

of the Côtes-du-Nord and Bernard's on sunny slopes determined the fundamental difference in their temperaments and works: Renan's spiritualism, Bernard's lucid thinking and exacting search for truth (RE 70). This theory of deterministic milieus, already developed by Sainte-Beuve and Hippolyte Taine, had been introduced in France by Mme de Staël, and even before that touched upon by Montesquieu.

A certain familiarity, then, with the Provençal countryside facilitates a better understanding of its poetic writers. "Ils ont poussé là-bas, au milieu des thyms et des lavandes, moitié Gascons et moitié Italiens, pleins de rêves paresseux et de menteries exquises. Ils ont du soleil dans le sang et des chants d'oiseaux dans la tête." (RN 212) To be more specific, Zola cites the case of Alphonse Daudet: "Son séjour en Algérie compléta sa naissance en Provence; des horizons de lumière s'ouvrirent, dont il a gardé l'éblouissement." (RN 213)

This dazzling light and heat from the sun appears in a Provençal setting in the opening scene of Daudet's *Numa Romestan* and conveys such realism to Zola that he claims to feel the sun in his own eyes (UC 314). But to Daudet's discredit, however, he has transformed the Provençal countryside repeatedly into the overly gentle one of the medieval troubadours. Zola only wishes that the severely realistic scrutiny which Daudet subjected his characters to had been equally applied to the natural surroundings. Zola's Provence differs sharply from Daudet's insistently gentle and friendly one; it should be "plus forte et plus brûlée, d'un parfum dont la violence tourne à l'amertume, sous la dureté de son azur sans nuage" (UC 315). Moreover, the Mistral for Zola is not the healthful and joyful gust of wind depicted by Daudet, but, on the contrary, a burning, roaring, destructive force capable of devastating an entire countryside. The Mistral, "angry" in Zola's *Le Docteur Pascal*, seems to "sweep away" not only the life the hero has shared with Clotilde, but also the very train that carries her off across the plains (271). On the other hand, the critic does approve of the "perfume of an ancient eclogue" (RN 239) that scents a scene of love in Daudet's *L'Arlésienne*, specifically the episode in which Vivette tries to seduce Frédéric beside the Vaccarès pond. Descriptions of Sunday strolls into the suburbs of Paris, which Zola cites in Daudet's *Fromont jeune et Risler aîné*, are frequently to be found in the works of Zola himself.

The portrayal of another walk in the outskirts of Paris attracts the critic's attention in *La Dévouée* of Léon Hennique, a fellow naturalist. Mood-setting descriptions of the suburbs, the setting sun, and falling dusk intersperse the recorded conversation of the strollers. In fact, this passage serves to illustrate a definition of a naturalistic work as being "une évocation intense de l'humanité et de la nature. On tâche de mettre un coin de la création dans une œuvre." (RE 195)

As for André Theuriet, another of Zola's contemporaries, the critic simply observes that the characters, though somewhat conventional, "prennent une véritable vie, sous les arbres, le long des allées profondes" (RN 284).

To be sure, these gleanings from Zola's essays on literary figures and their works regarding the relationship of man and nature may seem rather scanty and sometimes lacking in depth. But in all fairness to Zola, he does not devote a sustained and systematic study of man and nature *per se* in his critical works. Yet the naturalistic esthetic of that relationship resonates very clearly throughout, for it does form a part of the whole. In Zola's critical appraisal of French writers, his selective eye extracts that subject matter which supports and buttresses, whether positively or negatively, his literary biases. In his zeal to impose the naturalistic vision on his generation, sometimes Zola's magnifies or creatively distorts the view. Occasionally, a myopic overview of an author or a literary movement produces an erroneous premise. But all of these observations focus sharply on the constitution of the criteria for the naturalistic artist. Zola sheds further light for us on the relationship of man and nature when he pinpoints the principles of description and its techniques for naturalism.

Description for the naturalist, asserts Zola, is not the goal itself, but rather the means toward it, the study of man. Unlike the seventeenth-century's abstraction of him, man is in reality "une bête pensante, qui fait partie de la grande nature et qui est soumise aux multiples influences du sol où elle a poussé et où elle vit. C'est pourquoi un climat, un pays, un horizon, une chambre, ont souvent une importance décisive. Le romancier ne sépare donc plus le personnage de l'air où il se meut." (RE 122) Therefore, the naturalistic writer must emulate the zoologist who examines and describes the plant that nourishes the insect under study. Consequently, a character is never reduced to a psychological abstraction, but remains "un produit de l'air et du sol, comme la plante; c'est la conception scientifique" (RE 187). By defining description as "un état du milieu qui détermine et complète l'homme" (RE 187), Zola limits its use to revealing the human element.

He confesses, however, that the naturalists have not always maintained this desired equilibrium. The literary advent of naturalism, like all revolutionary movements, was of necessity initially violent and often excessive: "La nature est entrée dans nos œuvres d'un élan si impétueux, qu'elle les a emplies, noyant parfois l'humanité, submergeant et emportant les personnages, au milieu d'une débâcle de roches et de grands arbres." (RE 187) At the same time, Zola defends the documentary and instructive value of even the long descriptions; from them much worthwhile knowledge can be sifted, not to mention the actual matter available for future literary historians of naturalism.

The passion of these writers for nature often leads to inundations of animate and lengthy descriptions. Zola rationalizes that in Provence the exhilarating air and midday heat can so intoxicate the mind of an imaginative and poetic writer that he may depict images of singing brooks, chatting oaks, and sighing, bosom-shaped rocks; "nous avons rêvé d'élargir l'humanité et ... nous l'avons mise jusque dans les pierres des chemins" (RE 188-189). To illustrate the charge often raised against a number of naturalists for overlong descriptions, Zola refers to his own repetitive technique of terminating each of the five parts of *Une Page d'amour* by an extended descriptive passage of Paris, although the hour, season and atmospheric conditions change for each tableau, four of the five from the same window. Zola's portraits of Paris vie with Claude Monet's multiple paintings of the Rouen Cathedral at different hours of the day, and all painted from a single window, too. Hoewever, Zola states firmly, and perhaps defensively, that he is not indulging an urge to paint images profusely. Rather, he attributes his descriptive fervor, and that of his coterie to underlying "symphonic and human intentions" (RE 190).

In essence, then, Zola condemns all gratuitous description. The writer must not consider nature as a separate entity, but reveal how it relates to and determines man, how it affects him and brings about a change in his sentiments and actions.

II

RETURN TO NATURE

Noble terre, salut! Terre simple et naïve.

Musset

"Rousseau a le premier pleuré devant la nature" (DL 25) and, with those tears, aroused in his fellow man a longing to return to nature, too.

Prior to Rousseau's emotional outburst, the countryside was considered "dirty and in bad taste". The classical painter had to harmoniously rearrange and idealize his landscapes in order to correct and counteract the 'vulgar' sky and water. Artists architecturally reconstructed the elements of the countryside into majestic, noble monuments of academically acceptable lines and proportions. In his role as art critic, Zola praises "life" and "truth" for eventually "killing" this classical vision of nature.[1]

It was not until the advent of Camille Corot, Théodore Rousseau, and Jean-François Millet that nature appears depicted as it is rather than as the classical view would have it, according to the "Salon de 1875";[2] Zola credits Paul Huet, Corot, and Charles-François Daubigny in the "Exposition Universelle, 1878", for initiating the revolution in painting with their landscapes;[3] at another time the artist François-Louis Français and the novelist Paul de Kock were included among those who especially stimulated man's evolving enjoyment of the countryside in the nineteenth century (CN I 59); but, finally, in the "Salon de 1880", Zola settles upon four painters, namely Rousseau, Corot, Millet and Daubigny, as the most significant landscape artists who, through their "devotion to nature" and "search for truth", won the battle for naturalism in art by "returning to the eternal sources of observation and analysis".[4] They found their in-

---

[1] F. W. J. Hemmings and R. J. Niess, eds., *Émile Zola: Salons* (Paris: Minard, 1959), p. 133.
[2] Hemmings and Niess, p. 166.
[3] Hemmings and Niess, p. 217.
[4] Hemmings and Niess, pp. 252-253.

spiration in the simple landscapes on the outskirts of Paris, particularly in the woods of Boulogne and Vincennes. The popularity of their realistic paintings advanced man's general appreciation of nature. The landscape artists of Zola's period, "notre âge, qui s'est pris d'une tendre sympathie pour la nature", in the Salon de 1868, run about the countryside "en amants des rivières blanches et des vertes allées, s'intéressant au moindre bout d'horizon, peignant les brins d'herbe en frères attendris".[5]

In literature, Zola credits Rousseau, Chateaubriand, Lamartine and Musset for stimulating his literary contemporaries to seek fresh sensations in nature:

Nous promenons dans les champs notre système nerveux détraqué, impression-nés par le moindre souffle d'air.... La campagne vit pour nous, d'une vie poig-nante et fraternelle, et c'est pour cela que la vue d'un grand chêne, d'une haie d'aubépine, d'une tache de mousse nous émeut souvent jusqu'aux larmes.
...Ce respect et cette adoration de la nature sont à cette heure dans notre sang.[6]

In fact, Zola finds that the Parisians of his day have overdeveloped their taste for the countryside to the extent that they now feel "deprived of greenery" (CN I 55). He recounts how on Sundays working-class families walk for several kilometers to the outlying fortifications in order to satisfy, at least in part, this deprivation. From their vantage point they can gaze nostalgically beyond the bleak military zone and industrialized areas at the far-off green slopes, meadows, and trees miniaturized by the distance. This simple display of their "wretched passion" for open nature moves the author to pity. The city of Paris shares their desperate hunger for nature as it, too, looks "sans cesse à l'horizon, essoufflée, demandant du soleil et du vent" (CN I 62). The dismal aspects of urban existence intensify the city dweller's anxious feeling of alienation from nature. He nurtures a lifelong dream of possessing his own little retreat in the coun-try (CN I 55). In *La Terre* the Badeuils purchase the property called Rose-blanche with their savings of twenty-five years in order to realize their dream of "une vieillesse idyllique en pleine nature, avec des arbres, des fleurs, des oiseaux" (48).

Motives for man's return to nature abound.

The city is ugly. It lacks the beauty sought by its citizenry. A lonely scantiness, often defiled by filth and urban wastes, may characterize at times the bits of nature existing within the city proper. Two scenes from *L'Assommoir* illustrate this: In the first, the wedding party of Coupeau and Gervaise take refuge from a downpour under the Pont-Royal, beside

---

[5] Hemmings and Niess, p. 133.
[6] Hemmings and Niess, p. 240.

the polluted Seine. "Les dames étalèrent leurs mouchoirs sur les pavés, se reposèrent là, les genoux écartés, arrachant des deux mains les brins d'herbe poussés entre les pierres, regardant couler l'eau noire, comme si elles se trouvaient à la campagne…. L'averse avait cessé, mais la société se trouvait si bien, qu'elle ne songeait plus à s'en aller. La Seine charriait des nappes grasses, de vieux bouchons et des épluchures de légumes." (81)

The second scene, that of the reconciliation between Goujet and Gervaise, is unexpectedly set in an urban landscape scarcely appropriate to such an occasion. Goujet, who surprised Lantier trying to kiss Gervaise, fails to notice that he was holding her forcibly to the wall at the time. Gervaise, wishing to explain the true circumstances, pretends on the next day to be on an errand in the vicinity where Goujet works. As she passes the shop, the blacksmith joins her. They enter a large empty lot between factory buildings. A lone goat bleats in this pitiful remnant of nature that features patches of dead grass and a crumbling dead tree. Yet Gervaise remarks that it is like being in the country. Seated under the dead tree they glance upward at "le large ciel d'une pureté ardente", but the dazzling light redirects their gaze downward (260). Goujet finally broaches the subject bothering both, and Gervaise convinces him of what actually took place. Reassured, Goujet holds Gervaise's hand tightly in his own, and they lapse into silence. The author's more lyrical phrasing here reveals how their tenderness softens the scene about them. A small cloud formation, simply noted earlier, now glides slowly like a swan, while the goat bleats softly and mutedly in their direction. "Et, sans se lâcher les doigts, les yeux noyés d'attendrissement, ils se perdaient au loin, sur la pente de Montmartre blafard, …où les bouquets verts des cabarets borgnes les touchaient jusqu'aux larmes." (262) Before their reconciliation this distant greenery was simply qualified as "scanty".

One set of lovers enjoy a secluded natural setting beside the Seine in the very heart of Paris. Exploring some steep stairs along the western tip of the Ile Saint-Louis, Claude and Christine of L'Œuvre discover "une berge solitaire, plantée de grands arbres: et c'était un refuge délicieux, un asile en pleine foule, Paris grondant alentour, …pendant qu'ils goûtaient au bord de l'eau la joie d'être seuls, ignorés de tous. Dès lors, cette berge fut leur coin de campagne, le pays de plein air où ils profitaient des heures de soleil." (108) For the heroine of Une Page d'amour, the Passage des Eaux in Paris subtly shifts into a sylvan landscape. In the middle of the narrow, steep by-street of seven flights of steps, there is "le lit d'un ruisseau caillouté…. Les murs des jardins, à droite et à gauche, se renflaient, mangés d'une lèpre grise; des arbres allongeaient leurs branches, des feuillages pleuvaient, un lierre jetait la draperie de son épais manteau; et toutes ces verdures, qui ne laissaient voir que ces coins bleus de ciel, faisaient un jour verdâtre très doux et très discret. ...c'était un grand charme que cet escalier recueilli et ombragé, pareil à un chemin creux dans les forêts." (41) Also the private garden settings found in most of the novels represent retreats and refuges in nature.

The dirty-gray sunless sky which hangs heavily over Paris depresses and repulses some citizens. Two and a half years' exposure to it is more than the Charbonnels of *Son Excellence Eugène Rougon* can bear. The old man has had his fill of a town where one cannot see clearly in one's own room even in the middle of the afternoon. "Ce jour sale tombant du puits étroit de la cour, c'était Paris. Mais, Dieu merci! il allait retrouver le soleil, dans son jardin de Plassans." (207) The bleary sky that enshrouds Paris arouses in the heroine of *Nana* a need for the purity of nature. As day dawns on the close of one of her all-night parties, a bleak light blanches the windows. Nana looks out at the dismal awakening of the city beneath the soot-colored clouds that race across a livid sky. And, suddenly, she is overwhelmed by "un besoin de campagne, d'idylle, de quelque chose de doux et de blanc" (116).

Zola himself deplores the pallid Parisian sunlight and longs for "les clairs soleils, les midis ardents, éteints à jamais" (CN 275). His cry reaches its most strident pitch through his autobiographical figure in *La Confession de Claude*. Sitting alone in his cold, coffin-shaped garret, Claude recalls the warm Provençal summer evenings when he and boy-hood friends discussed future plans. The Parisian garret they romanticized then differs greatly from his own miserable hovel which bars entry to the sun. Claude cries out nostalgically for his fields, streams, and sunsets. Even a sumptuous apartment could not lure him to remain in Paris now. "Je préfère le luxe de Dieu au luxe des hommes." (14)

A second prime motive for man's wish to return to nature is prompted by urban encroachment on freedom of movement. As man proceeds away from the constrained streets hemmed in by buildings into the more open areas of the city, he senses physical and mental liberation. In *L'Œuvre*, Claude Lantier and three friends enter easily into a passionate exchange of ideas as they stride, four abreast, along the broad tree-lined Boulevard des Invalides, somewhat removed from the hubbub of the city. Their discussion attains its greatest zeal with their arrival at the spacious esplanade stretching far and fanning out widely before them. They are delighted by its calm expanses which provide ample space for magnanimous and energetic gesticulation (76).

Clorinde Delestang, in *Son Excellence Eugène Rougon*, experiences a somewhat similar release from the constricting pressures of the cramped city. She accompanies her husband and Rougon to a meeting of ministers at Saint-Cloud. Pressed for time, Rougon has his coachman take a short-cut through the narrow streets of the Chaillot district. Only when the landau brings them onto the graveled road at the Porte de la Muette where the horizon reveals the green grounds and budding trees of the Bois de Boulogne, does Clorinde stretch out and remark that now they can breathe and chat (296-297). The hero of *La Confession de Claude* has difficulty in breathing inside a stuffy Parisian dance hall, and he yearns for the cool outdoor dance floors of Provence (46).

The city air is particularly oppressive for Denise in the large department store where she is employed as a salesgirl, in *Au Bonheur des dames*. As she anticipates a Sunday excursion to Joinville with friends, "elle étouffait, prise d'un besoin de plein ciel, rêvant de grandes herbes où elle entrait jusqu'aux épaules, d'arbres géants dont les ombres coulaient sur elle comme une eau fraîche. Son enfance, passée dans les verdures grasses du Cotentin, s'éveillait, avec le regret du soleil." (149) Early that Sunday morning, as Denise and her friends look for a fiacre to take them to the railroad station, the warm May sun dissipates all thoughts of the store. Already she projects herself into the open countryside, "et c'était comme une nouvelle santé, une joie infinie, où elle entrait avec des sensations neuves de gamine" (150).

A third, and often companion motive for the desire in man to return to nature is apparent in the preceding example. Not only is the city sordid and cramped, but it is also unhealthful. In the outline of *Le Ventre de Paris*, Zola stresses the necessity of giving a fairly important role to a widowed farmer, who will represent the "healthful and noble" aspects of production in contrast with the indigestible character of consumption, symbolized by Les Halles:

Je me ménage un échappé sur la campagne. Un jour, la fermière emmène Charles [Florent] et mon petit peintre à la campagne, dans sa voiture.
Sensations de Charles. Il est ravi de ne plus entendre les grondements de la Halle. Il est dans le trou heureux où la nourriture se fabrique. Comparaison. Mettre cela au milieu de l'œuvre, pour produire une opposition. (342)

Mme François has invited Florent and Claude to spend a day at her farm. They meet at the small barnyard in Paris where she keeps her horse while selling her vegetables at Les Halles. Her wagon, now loaded with cabbage leaves to be used as fertilizer, is like "un avant-goût de la campagne, en plein Paris" (215). Claude and Florent lie on top of the leaves as Mme François drives the wagon up Rue de Rivoli and the Champs-Elysées. While the others converse, Florent remains silent, watches the rose hue of dawn lighten the sky, and happily anticipates leaving Les Halles far behind for the pure air of the country (217). Arriving at the Arc de Triomphe, Florent smells the scent of grass, sits up, and turns his back on Paris to look at the countryside beyond.

The heroine of *L'Assommoir* wishes she, too, could turn her back on Paris. One bitterly cold evening, as the poverty-stricken and starving Gervaise walks along the streets, she passes by a railroad yard. A departing train disappears into what she imagines is the open countryside where her life might begin anew, far from her present squalid existence in the city (427-428). She laughs at her long vanished hopes to retire to the country, knowing now that the only plot of green that awaits her is at the cemetery (438).

An entire national body felt compelled to turn its back on Paris. As the Prussian army was advancing toward the capital in 1871, the Assemblée Nationale decided to move to Versailles. A far better choice, writes Zola at the time, would have been Barbizon, a very small town close to nature. "Ah! messieurs, quel retour à l'âge d'or! Vos séances, tenues dans une clairière, se seraient passées sous l'œil de Dieu même, dans le soleil bienfaisant d'avril. Et quelle sincérité, quelle pureté, quelle simplicité d'âme, en pleine nature! Vous avez vraiment laissé échapper une belle occasion de délibérer loin du tumulte des villes, à l'abri des foules malfaisantes." (M 53)

The unwholesome atmosphere of the city contrasts explicitly with the salutary country air in the short story "Lili". The author depicts Ninon, in opposition to the worldly Lili, as a robust child of nature who grew up freely and vigorously like a wild plant in the wholesome open air and fields. Returning from a ball, Ninon points to the wilting flowers in her bouquet: her fate would be similar were she transplanted permanently into the stuffy air of the urban environs they just left. She is no hothouse plant (CN 344). Zola then relates that on one spring afternoon, while seated on a park bench in the Tuileries, he observed the studied coquetry of a seven-year old child named Lili in company with a little girl friend. Their behavior approximated that of urbane Parisian ladies of polite society. Upon noticing the author's old-fashioned hat, the girls broke into laughter; but like proper women who frequent salons, each held a hand to her mouth. Embarrassed, the author fled, and now pleads in tones reminiscent of Rousseau: "Ah! Ninon, Ninon, emmène-moi ces demoiselles

dans les fermes, habille-les de toile grise et laisse-les se rouler dans la mare
où barbottent les canards. Elles reviendront bêtes comme des oies, saines
et vigoureuses comme de jeunes arbres." (CN 348)

The city, then, is corrupt. Nature alone holds purity. Most sadly, urban
society harbors the fallen woman. Love in a natural setting is pure; in the
city, it is venal. This is a dominant theme in *La Confession de Claude*. The
hero places the girl of one's dreams in nature. In one of his letters from
Paris he asks: "Frères, n'avez-vous jamais rêvé qu'un soir d'automne
vous rencontriez dans les blés une brune fille de seize ans?" (17). Perhaps
this question is an oversight on the part of Zola, because in an earlier
letter Claude reminded his friends of how they nurtured visions of viva-
cious and laughing brunettes while he envisaged for himself a pale, blond
ethereal creature (12-13). She somewhat resembles Fleur-des-eaux of the
short story "Simplice", the undine who can lightly float away on a moon-
beam. This evanescent quality is characteristic of the beautiful girls whom
Sandoz, another autobiographical figure, in *L'Œuvre*, had cherished in his
adolescent dreams. These beings would spring out of the woods to spend
the day with him only to fade into the shadows at twilight (40).

However, the girl of Claude's dreams never materializes. Instead, he
falls in love with Laurence, a Parisian prostitute. On the first spring day
they commence a long walk away from the city. At the fortifications they
wander contentedly for a while down among the trenches whose limited
horizons exclude signs of the city and include only a view of stones, grass,
and sky. This foretaste of nature, though attenuated in form, restimulates
their need to reach open country. They proceed through the disheartening
Montrouge area at the edge of the city, where man has lacerated and
slaughtered the natural scene in the name of industrial progress. Shortly
after hastening from there, the lovers find themselves in another area
where civilization again desecrates and defiles nature. It is a small valley
through which runs the thick, sluggish, slimy, stinking stream of the
Bièvre. The river is nothing but a nauseous sewer into which the tanneries
empty their acrid wastes, and a hilltop hospital its pollution. The polluted
stream seems to mirror the couple's present relationship, one that Claude
seeks anxiously to amend. He notices that Laurence has reassumed her
customary bored and blank expression, her smile at the beginning of the
walk having long since disappeared. "...j'ai compris qu'il fallait à cette
âme endormie plus de soleil, une nature plus douce pour lui rendre ses
quinze ans." (81) Therefore, Claude leads her deeper into the countryside,
"in quest of the young and virginal spring" (81). They find it on an isolated
grassy clearing in the woods, which transfers, at least momentarily, its

virginity to Laurence. We will delve, in the next chapter, into this concept of nature transferring virginity to the fallen woman.

The hero of *L'Œuvre* seeks out nature, too, to beautify his sexual relationship with Christine. The intimacy was initiated in the dull light of dusk in his studio. The next morning Claude feels a need to take her far away from Paris into the sunny countryside (153). By train and ferry they travel to Bennecourt where they have lunch. Then they walk beyond the village into a thick oak grove. "C'était le bout du monde qu'ils cherchaient l'un et l'autre, un gazon d'une douceur de velours, un abri de feuilles, où le soleil seul pénétrait, en minces flèches de flamme." (155) And, immediately, they give themselves to each other. As they emerge from the woods afterwards, they meet Père Poirette who shows them a house for rent, with apricot trees and giant rosebushes blooming in front and a small potato garden in the rear. Its isolation in a natural setting has great appeal for the two lovers. Some weeks later they decide to move there. Claude yearns eagerly for "good nature", its promise of "great tranquillity", and its provision of true atmospheric conditions for his future landscape paintings (157).

"Good nature" also attracts men to partake of its solitude and to till its soil. They are motivated to return to nature because they find civilized society evil. In several instances, soldiers abandon military life for the farm. In the short story "Le Sang", each of four professional soldiers recounts in turn his terrifying nightmare, precipitated by the bloody slaughter upon the battlefield. When the morning trumpet sounds the departure for the troops, the four soldiers decide to have their sleep troubled no longer by the ghosts of those they have slain. They bury their rifles, bathe in the river, and arm in arm go off in search of farm labor. These former soldiers and future tillers of the soil have their counterpart in the hero of "Les Quatre journées de Jean Gourdon" and also in Jean Macquart of the *Rougon-Macquart* series. The latter, a veteran of two wars, seeks, after each cessation of hostilities, to renew direct contact with the earth, first after the war in the Crimea in *La Terre* and a second time after the Franco-Prussian war in *La Débâcle* and *Le Docteur Pascal*.

Before the protagonist in the short story about Jean Gourdon completes his military service, he receives a letter from his uncle pleading that he return to the farm and the rewarding, cheerful work with the soil (CN 444). Jean does so and, in turn, on the day that his wife bears him a son, hopes the child will carry on the family tradition of remaining on the land that has given them great peace (CN 458).

Jean Macquart does not find such peace in the country in *La Terre*, a novel that counters, in some measure, the earlier romantic idealism. Although he finds the earth both beautiful and good, he discovers that he must contend with a basic meanness of the peasants. At one point in this strongly antiromantic depiction of peasant life, an ironic barb is directed at that literature which overidealizes the life of the peasant. To the Fouans and other neighbors assembled in Fouans' stable, Jean reads aloud from *Les Malheurs et le triomphe de Jacques Bonhomme*, a book prop- agandizing Bonapartism. One passage counsels the laborer not to move from his village into the city where one spends all his money for the necessities of life and useless luxuries. Those who work in the city either seek diversion in the country or dream of retiring there. Consequently, the villagers and peasants are reminded that they already possess true happi- ness in their healthful work on the fields in the sunny open air (84). While the city-bred Jean is moved by this idyll of rustic life, the poor wretched peasants with their weather-beaten faces wonder whether the book ridi- cules them.

Satire punctuates the theme of return to nature more boldly in one youthful work. Before the two heroes of the "Aventures du grand Sidoine et du petit Médéric" set out on their persistent search for the utopian Royaume des Heureux, a talkative bullfinch tells Médéric how Princess Primevère has established an animal reserve for the peaceful coexistence of beasts and birds. The author suspects that the bullfinch has fled from the reserve because of a preference for "sun and brambles" over the monotonous universal diet of milk given to all of the animals (CN 231). In this instance, the desire to return to nature is prompted by an artificially created animal civilization that has stifled the inherent instincts of its citizenry. The young heroes eventually find the kingdom with its wildlife refuge. When the giant Sidoine kills with one blow of his gargantuan fist the stronger beasts who devoured the weaker ones in their common uprising, Médéric explains that the stronger were simply following their animal instinct. Regretting this destructive use of his fists, Sidoine re- solves to think no more but instead to work and sleep in the sun and to fight constructively with only the earth (CN 265).

The image of a giant battling the soil reappears in *Son Excellence Eugène Rougon*, whose hero nourishes an ambitious project to incorpo- rate a large section of the Landes in an effort to found a private small empire. He envisages himself manually reconverting its marshy lands into fertile soil. Envisioning himself grown to prodigious proportions, his fists crush stones, his shoulders bear houses, and a single kick excavates a river bed (158).

Thus far, man has sought to flee from the ugly, cramped, sordid, corrupt, venal, evil and unhealthful city in search of the beauty, freedom, purity and wholesomeness of nature. Many of the flights, however, will remain only flights of the mind. Often they are only escapes into the past, dreams for the future or even an idle daydream, as in one of the "Souvenirs". Zola, while watching baggage-filled cabs rumble to various railroad stations, despairs at having to remain in Paris, especially when he imagines one truck destined for some protected spot along the rocky shore near Marseilles, another bound for the green environs of Normandy. As he reflects upon all the past spring seasons of confinement within his urban 'dungeon', his desire "for foliage and open skies" grows to painful intensity (CN 380). This desire is not unmingled with sensuousness, for he wishes that he could make himself sufficiently small to crawl into the trunk of clothes belonging to a certain lady in a rose-colored hat who rides past in the direction of the Gare de Lyon. No doubt she is on her way to Marseilles and a certain isolated marine setting secluded beside the lapping waves of the sea where, "a hundred leagues from imbeciles", they could safely undress before swimming and acting like youngsters again (CN 381).

Frequently, through reminiscing, Zola escapes into the past and the sunny Provençal countryside, explicitly as the author himself in his prefaces to the Contes à Ninon and the Nouveaux Contes à Ninon, or vicariously through the autobiographical characters of the hero of La Confession de Claude or Pierre Sandoz in L'Œuvre. In the prefaces to the two volumes of tales addressed to Ninon, the author recalls carefree times spent with her in the Provençal countryside. The human being, freed in the midst of nature, becomes acutely aware of the vital forces at work in the universe. "Nos courses de gamins échappés, nos amours d'oiseaux libres, m'avaient inspiré un grand mépris du monde, une tranquille croyance aux seules énergies de la vie." (CN 274)

This "great contempt for society" is restated as a "hatred of the city" in an autobiographically inspired passage from L'Œuvre where the city exerts restrictions on the youthful freedom that Zola and his boyhood friends had enjoyed in Provence. Claude and Sandoz reminisce over their escapades with Louis Dubuch in sunny Provence. During school holidays the three youths spent days at a stretch wandering about the countryside. "C'étaient des fuites loin du monde, une absorption instinctive au sein de la bonne nature, une adoration irraisonnée de gamins pour les arbres, les eaux, les monts, pour cette joie sans limite d'être seuls et d'être libres." (37) They swam and hunted. Often while Claude sketched a landscape,

Sandoz recited poems by Hugo or Musset. Sometimes, the boys would act out, beside a stream, a drama by one of these two romantics until night-fall. Instead of succumbing to the easy life of the small town, they scaled "les collines voisines pour y découvrir des solitudes ignorées, déclamant des vers sous des pluies battantes, sans vouloir d'abri, par haine des cités" (39).[7] A Rousseauistic posture strongly radiates here and in the longer quotation cited above it.

In a letter that reveals a nostalgic attempt to return to nature by way of memory, the hero of *La Confession de Claude* reminds his 'brothers' of their boyhood excursions into nature. He recognizes their "healthy debauchery for the fields" as a kind of madness (65). He cherishes the memories of predawn sorties in search of game, even though they generally returned empty-handed. Claude writes that the geographical distance from Paris does not separate him from that open sun-drenched country-side because its landscapes have imprinted themselves indelibly upon his mind (64).

Some mental flights to nature are triggered by auditory, olfactory, and visual associations. A hymn conveys the hero of *La Faute de l'abbé Mou-ret* to a nature setting. The star Venus evokes the priest's adoration of the Virgin Mary, and he begins to chant "Ave maris stella". This hymn mentally conveys him to the distant blue beaches of a calm sea lit by a huge "smiling" star (106).

That olfactory and visual associations transport man to a natural setting is best exemplified by the sensitivity of Florent in *Le Ventre de Paris*. A market of herbs and spices pervades the morning air with such pungency that Florent momentarily believes himself to be on a hillside in the country (31). On another occasion it is the sea odor from the fish stalls in Les Halles which projects him to a bay on the Guianean seacoast where the outgoing tide leaves behind the strong scent of seaweed steam-ing under a blazing sun (109). Each evening as Florent looks down from the height of his garret window, the sea of roofs of the numerous pavilions of Les Halles below conjure "la vision vague d'un bord de mer, avec les eaux mortes et ardoisées d'une baie à peine frissonnantes du roulement lointain de la houle. Il s'oubliait, il rêvait chaque soir une côte nouvelle." (125) Weather and seasonal changes transform the roofs into a variety of

---

[7] It is in an essay on Musset that Zola elaborates on the autobiographical details (DL 73-75). There he recounts how he, as a sixteen-year old youth, and his friends felt the need for the great outdoors, how the activities of their escapades into nature would vary according to the season of the year, and how they first recited Hugo's poems only to abandon them a year later for Musset's.

waterscapes, and, invariably, through an association of images, Florent is transported to some distant scene of nature. "Et lui, à chaque aspect de cet horizon changeant, s'abandonnait à des songeries tendres ou cruelles; la neige le calmait, l'immense drap blanc lui semblait un voile de pureté jeté sur les ordures des Halles; les nuits limpides, les ruissellements de lune, l'emportaient dans le pays féerique des contes. Il ne souffrait que par les nuits brûlantes de juin, qui étalaient le marais nauséabond, l'eau dormante d'une mer maudite." (288-289) But any evocation of a pleasant natural setting is quickly wiped from Florent's mind whenever the indigestive monstrous "belly" of Les Halles belches its foul breath upon the city of Paris.

Similarly, the glasswork of the central gallery of the large Parisian department store in *Au Bonheur des dames* changes into a distant seascape for Denise and Deloche. From a vantage point just under the roofs of the tall building, the two employees look down at the "lake" of glass whose edges resemble rocky coasts (362). Their conversation about the green countryside around Valognes, near the Normandy coast, gradually fades as a mirage of the rich pasture lands of the Cotentin peninsula bathed in the luminous marine haze appears in the sunny glass lake below them (363). Auditory associations reinforce the visual as the department store vibrates with its teeming life and muffled noises which now sound to the couple like the ocean wind passing over the plants and through the trees (363).

There are also dreams, nightmares, and hallucinations that can transport a character to a setting in nature. One of the protagonists in the short story "Le Sang" retreats in a dream to a peaceful, virginal world. Elberg raptly envisages the earth in its infancy, a world where harmony reigns among all living creatures. Here, he feels himself become "stronger and better" (CN 117). (Purification and physical rejuvenation, phenomena that often occur when Zola's characters come into direct contact with nature, will be examined at length in the next chapter.) Elberg likens his refreshing dream-entry into virginal nature, a welcome escape from the slaughter on the battlefield, to the "delightful sensation" felt by the miner who remounts into the fresh air (CN 117). Lisa of *Le Ventre de Paris* experiences a similar sensation. In the heat and amid the rank odors of the underground poultry coops, Marjolin tries to seduce Lisa, but she hits him so forcefully between the eyes that his skull strikes the corner of a slaughtering-block, knocking him senseless. As she climbs up into the brightness of day, Lisa senses great relief (212). The sensation of liberation that accompanies escape from subterranean depths is, of course, a central image in *Germinal*. Twice the protagonist of the short story "La Mort d'Olivier Bécaille" senses this release: once when he awakens from a nightmare in which he struggles through a subterranean passage, and later as he escapes from the coffin in which he is actually buried alive.

During the delirium of his bout with typhoid fever Zola himself had imagined vividly the horror of being buried alive, coupled with the dire need to reach the open air of nature. The young author recalls in "Le Printemps — journal d'un convalescent" (written in 1858 or 1859 and placed in the appendix of *La Faute de l'abbé Mouret*), when first recovering from his illness, the impression of having spent months near death "in the bottom of a dark vault" (LFAM 427). As the sun sets on his first day of feeble convalescence, he feels his life sink with the sun and fears he will hear again passing footsteps on his grave (LFAM 429). The sun remains hidden on succeeding days. The overcast ashen sky deeply depresses him, and a recurring siege of fever thrusts him into an endless fall down a black void. Eventually he finds himself ensnared in a nightmare of ceaseless crawling through low, narrow, interminable subterranean passages deep within the earth. At times the passages close in on him, necessitating a tremendous struggle to work his way through the earth. Only his intuition that the passage must ultimately open out onto a "wide, limpid and calm horizon" goads him on to continued efforts (LFAM 431).

In *Germinal* the nightmare becomes an actuality. A dream of a sunny landscape will afford Catherine temporary respite from terror, and her escape will seem even more real during her subsequent delirium. Flooding waters rise gradually toward Etienne and Catherine who are trapped in the mine. As the black waters reach the feet of the sleeping Catherine, Etienne decides not to awaken her from a possible "dream of open air and life in the sun" (518). (A similar dream goads the mine horse, Bataille, to dash so wildly through the mine in search of the sun and nature of younger days that he destroys himself.) Deprived of light and food for many days, Etienne and Catherine's physical senses deceive them. This is especially true in the case of Catherine: "Les bourdonnements de ses oreilles étaient devenus des murmures d'eau courante, des chants d'oiseaux; et elle sentait un violent parfum d'herbes écrasées, et elle voyait clair, de grandes taches jaunes volaient devant ses yeux, si larges, qu'elle se croyait dehors, près du canal, dans les blés, par une journée de beau soleil." (529) This is one of the rare descriptions in the novel of a landscape that is not desolate.

Hallucination transplants Catherine into the midst of nature in the same manner as delirium tremens does for Coupeau, committed to the asylum at Sainte-Anne, in *L'Assommoir*. He strolls about his padded cell as though he were in the Bois de Vincennes and deeply breathes in what he thinks is the spray-drenched air from the surrounding fountains and cascades of water (444).

At times, a very vivid imagination is as powerful as hallucination to transport one into nature. The hero of *La Confession de Claude* claims he has the faculty to experience simultaneously two parallel existences: the physical and the spiritual. While his physical being remains continuously sensitive to outer reality, his mind can suppress that reality, when unpleasant, to a subordinate plane, and thus permit him to live spiritually elsewhere under more ideal conditions: "Tandis que je m'avance sous la pluie, en pleine boue, tandis que j'ai énergiquement conscience de tout le froid, de toute l'humidité, je puis, par une faculté étrange, faire luire le soleil, avoir chaud, me créer un ciel doux et tendre, sans cesser de sentir le ciel noir qui pèse à mes épaules." (88)

However, this ability to function concurrently on two planes can also cause him to swing like a pendulum between the two, with the result that his ultra-terrestrial experiences accentuate the more his true miserable existence. When thrust too far into the imaginative, the subsequent confrontation with reality only plunges Claude into deeper dejection. For example, he escapes momentarily from his dark and humid garret into a happy remembrance of the early spring excursion spent with Laurence in the sunny Fontenay woods and of the rejuvenating effect of nature upon her; but then his sadness and deception are intensified when he sees the apathetic Laurence dozing before him in the midst of their squalid quarters (89). These oscillations from a cheerless reality to a radiant memory and back to an even more depressing reality have their roots in an experience which Zola expresses in a letter in 1860, five years before the publication of the novel. He informs Paul Cézanne of his monotonous existence in Paris where he writes amid dreary surroundings, only occasionally brightened by the recall of some happy moment spent in Provence. The evocation of a pleasant experience from the past usually occurs after a ray of sunlight strikes his window to remind him of nature beyond. Then he leans back in his chair, closes his eyes, and imagines himself with his friends in Provence. "Puis tout s'évanouit, la réalité revient plus terrible, je reprends ma plume et je me sens des envies de pleurer." (C 64)

For a lover, imagination sometimes takes the form of a conscious dream that projects him and his beloved into the future and into a natural setting. In addressing Ninon, the short story writer says that many years later he will expect to find her "dans les campagnes tièdes encore de nos

tendresses" (CN 280). He suggests that after they meet by a certain haw-
thorne bush, Ninon will lead him on a pilgrimage to each of their memory-
filled haunts about the countryside.

Generally, however, the lover's daydream of the future is motivated by
a wish to uplift the sentimental relationship with the girl he loves. The
hero of *La Confession de Claude* relies on nature to effectuate a transformation in Laurence. Unable to elicit love from her in their sordid
Parisian milieu, Claude suggests that they go to Provence for "une vie
d'amour sur cette terre ardente qui te rendra ta jeunesse et te donnera une
beauté sombre, passionnée" (114). There, he claims, they will live and
love, and forget the past; "le présent seul, avec son grand soleil, sa nature
féconde, ses amours fortes et douces, existera pour nos cœurs" (114).

Daniel, in *Le Vœu d'une morte*, also places future trust in nature to
resolve his dilemma. He recognizes his inability to change Jeanne Tellier's shallow character as long as she remains in contact with Parisian
society and its superficial pleasures. But his hopes rise when he learns that
he will spend the summer with the Tellier family in the country. His joy is
twofold: he is happy at the prospect of returning to nature, and he hopefully places his trust in the latter to correct Jeanne's selfish ways (92).

But each hero, thwarted in love and in effecting with the aid of nature
the desired lasting change in his beloved, returns alone to a natural scene
for self-rejuvenation. On two different occasions Daniel flees to Saint-
Henri to seek the solace of the sea. The first flight follows Jeanne's
marriage to Lorin, the second occurs after he unwittingly brings together
his best friend Georges and Jeanne, a meeting that leads to her second
marriage.

Claude, disappointed in love, concludes his writings with the announce-
ment that he is about to rejoin his friends in Provence where he looks forward to the beneficent rejuvenation that the Provençal countryside can
render him.

Je veux puiser une nouvelle jeunesse dans nos larges horizons, dans notre soleil
ardent et pur.... Nous irons dans les plaines, au bord de la rivière ombreuse;
nous reprendrons la vie de nos seize ans, et j'oublierai ainsi l'année terrible
que je viens de vivre.... Je redeviendrai jeune.... Attendez-moi, et faites que
la Provence soit plus douce, plus encourageante pour me recevoir et me rendre
mon enfance. (139-140)[8]

[8] Three years before publication of this novel, Zola addressed a letter from Paris to
Paul Cézanne and Jean-Baptistin Baille, his good friends from school days, in which he
looks forward to spending a brief vacation with them in the sunny Provençal countryside (C 228).

The natural setting into which the hero attempts to project himself and his beloved is often idyllic. Yet these imaginative flights into nature are rarely brought to fruition and, consequently, lead to further frustration.

From a very early age, Guillaume, in *Madeleine Férat*, nurtured the dream of sharing a peaceful retreat in the country with some compassionate being, whether lover or comrade, who would give him the kind of tender love denied him at home and school. Eventually he meets Madeleine whom he wishes to take deep into the "intimate countryside" near La Noiraude, his father's large estate. When she moves into a cottage nearby, facilitating clandestine trysts in the woods, Guillaume's childhood dream materializes. As a young schoolboy, "il avait rêvé une solitude heureuse, un coin perdu et caché au fond duquel il passerait de longues journées oisives, ... caressé ... par quelque bonne et douce fée qui resterait toujours près de lui; et plus tard, à dix-huit ans, lorsque des désirs vagues commençaient à battre dans ses veines, il avait repris ce songe sous les arbres du parc, aux bords des eaux claires, remplaçant la fée par une amoureuse, courant les taillis, avec l'espoir de rencontrer sa chère tendresse à chaque détour des sentiers." (68) Each spring following their marriage, Guillaume and Madeleine scurry about the countryside to revisit their favorite spots.

One day Guillaume brings home his old friend Jacques, only to learn from Madeleine that he was her former lover. Consequently, Guillaume and Madeleine take flight toward Paris, stopping overnight at an inn in Mantes. There Guillaume articulates his unceasing need for an isolated retreat in nature: "J'ai toujours fait le songe de vivre au désert, et bien des fois j'ai cherché dans la campagne quelque trou perdu pour m'y enfouir." (191)

This last image may express a repressed desire to return to the womb rather than, or perhaps fused with, a death wish, when it is considered in relation with two recurrent dreams during his youth. Each suggests a desire to return to a prenatal state of suspension. Before Jacques began to protect Guillaume from the beatings inflicted by fellow classmates, Guillaume would lie awake at night in the dormitory conjuring images of solitary landscapes. When he was tormented, the prevalent tableau evoked was of a rocky, yawning chasm where torrents roared down deep gorges and eagles slowly circled high overhead. There, on a white slab at the edge of the abyss the dreamer found himself "assis et comme mort, au milieu de la désolation et de la nudité de l'horizon" (195). A repressed wish for death fuses here with one to return to the womb. Preceding the simile 'like dead', the adjective 'seated' describes a body posture that is ordinarily associated with the living and that probably approaches, because of the flat surface of the slab, the fetal position. 'Desolation' apposes 'nudity', a noun which, though it may mean barren, often connotes human warmth and sensuousness. Both repressed wishes afford the dreamer a quiescent state of being to offset the conscious unpleasant experiences of the day. Only the repressed wish to return to the womb remains discernible when the boy, in a calmer mood, dreamed of a tiny island, "jetée au sein d'un large fleuve tranquille", whose distant green banks appeared faded in the white vapors of mist. On this island, amid voluptuous natural surroundings, he imagined himself "couché sur l'herbe molle, bercé par la grande voix sourde et continue du fleuve, rafraîchi par les souffles gras de cette nature humide" (195). It was his ambition then to join a band of roving gypsies and find those peaceful and consoling landscapes. And, now, the adult Guillaume proposes that he and Madeleine set off in search of these vistas which he still believes must exist in reality somewhere.

The nomadic existence of gypsies, whom Guillaume envied for their happy existence in the sun (194), also has a strong appeal for the heroine of *Thérèse Raquin*. She confides to her lover Laurent that she often wished to lead the carefree life of a gypsy in the open air: "J'avais des besoins cuisants de grand air." (38)

In *Une Page d'amour*, imaginative flights into nature also assume idealistic dimensions. Dr. Henri Deberle assures Hélène Grandjean that her daughter is convalescing well and should be able to go down into the garden in another two weeks. He tells Hélène how the flowers have blossomed out all over the garden; in silence they gaze tenderly at each other, "et leur pensée commune les promenait tous deux dans les allées profondes, des allées idéales, noires d'ombre et où tombaient des pluies de roses" (173). Later, another doctor suggests that Mme Grandjean take her daughter to Italy in the spring. Hélène relates her plans to the Deberles, and Mme Deberle replies that, by coincidence, she had spoken that very morning of going to Naples. She proposes now that the two families visit Italy together. And while she prattles on about the itinerary, Hélène and Henri envisage themselves as lovers strolling together in the "ideal spring" of Italy (307).

A purely idealistic dream within *Le Rêve* is proposed by Félicien, whose father refuses to permit him to marry Angélique. Learning that Angélique is extremely ill, Félicien climbs up to the balcony and enters her bedroom. He tries to persuade her to leave with him that very night by carriage to some far-distant country where they can love one another in leisure and peace. Within the walls of a large enclosed garden where springtime is eternal, flowers grow as "tall as trees", and fruits taste "sweeter than honey", their love will flourish, too (177). A less naive but more poignant dream does materialize, although short-lived, in the "Souvenirs", in the episode that relates Jacques' love for Madeleine who has not long to live. Wishing to fill her remaining life with undivided love, Jacques retreats with her to a country cottage where she lives on for two more years, cultivating the roses that "grow like weeds" there (CN 420).

An early death cuts short the fleeting happiness of not only these last named heroines but also that of Albine, in *La Faute de l'abbé Mouret*, who takes her own life when nature fails to reconvert the priest to the dogma of its living forces. After the idyllic interlude in the Paradou, Albine goes to the church to persuade Abbé Mouret to leave behind this thing he calls God, who loves him less than does she, and to return with her to recommence their love, happiness, and freedom in the midst of the abundant life in the Paradou (331). After Albine's departure from the church, Serge begins to think more and more about her and their happy existence together in the Paradou. He recalls that the park had so sharpened his physical sensitivity that "sa première jeunesse ... lui apparaissait toute noire, passée loin du soleil, ingrate, blême, infirme" (349). But the Paradou, the Provençal rendering of "paradise", is powerless to restimulate him on his return there. The paradise gained by him as a man is lost to him as the Abbé Mouret.

The earthly paradise of nature is seldom regained by the characters in the examples examined thus far. Most of the mental flights from society to nature remain fancies: idle daydreams, wishful thoughts, future hopes, nostalgic reminiscences, sensory-induced images, pleasant dreams, hallucinations, anxiety-filled nightmares, or deeply-buried delirium.

Yet the desire to return to nature is deeply rooted within all these characters, and more so in those who have grown up close to nature. In these longings, the individual not only feels an intimacy with nature, but also seeks absorption in a maternal nature. At times that desire to return to the bosom of Mother Nature appears to be a repressed wish to return to the mother herself.

Most often man's fervent desire to return to nature is motivated by an urgent need to escape from some disagreeable or painful aspect of civilization. Some of Zola's characters simply seek a view of greenery or sun or clean air, that is, flight from the drab, cold, or stifling atmosphere of the city. Others seek the open countryside to give free expression to an almost childlike unbounded freedom, which is, in part, flight from the restrictions imposed by the community of man upon the liberty of the individual. Several seek a spring landscape, each in the hope that its purity and virginity might cleanse his beloved of certain moral impurities, that is to say, flight from the corruption and artificiality found in or imposed by society. Many seek a solitary spot in the bosom of nature to share with a beloved being, representing flight from a collective whole. Some seek an idyllic natural setting to share with a loved one, namely, flight from cultural mores. And still others seek the solitude of the peasants' earth, in effect, flight from the barbaric wars of civilization.

III

PURIFICATION AND PACIFICATION OF MAN

> ...je sens la paix de la grande nature
> Qui m'entre dans le cœur.
>
> Hugo

In his return to nature, man trusts that nature will exorcise and purify him. He seeks various kinds of purification when he takes flight from the city with its sordid ugliness, its cramped confinement, its disease-breeding atmosphere, its corruption and venality. Purification is sought on physical, psychological, and spiritual planes. To what extent can nature cleanse man of evil, moral corruption, sickness, anxiety and despair, negative emotions and tense states of being?

The act of purification in nature usually takes place in sunny settings, such as Zola knew as a youth. His fiction, when written in the cold damp gloom of Paris, attests at times to his own personal need for the luminous spring landscapes, especially those of Provence. When Zola places a character in a cheerful setting, his style acquires added exuberance and seems to reveal the author's vicarious enjoyment in the character's recaptured youth, in a paradise regained.

Youth regained in the presence of nature generally implies a certain purification of being at the same time. In *La Confession de Claude* the hero states: "A chaque printemps, mon cœur rajeunit, ma chair devient plus légère. Il y a purification de tout mon être." (78) Guillaume of *Madeleine Férat* "se purifia de sa vie de collège" when he adopts the solitary life close to nature at La Noiraude (59). The sea breeze is equally cleansing for Lazare Chanteau of *La Joie de vivre* upon returning home after his first year of studies in Paris: "La rude brise de mer le lavait des odeurs du quartier latin." (51) In creating the pasty-faced, fat Pauline from Paris for that same novel, Zola stipulates in his outline that "à l'air de la mer, elle se desempâtera, prendra de la force, deviendra belle, ...la bonté sera sur sa figure" (371). Purification of another sort is rendered in *L'Assommoir*. Breathing the salutary country air, Coupeau, continually inebriated

in Paris, remains completely sober during the three months that he works
as a farm hand. Zola marvels: "On ne se doute pas combien ça désaltère
les pochards de quitter l'air de Paris, où il y a dans les rues une vraie
fumée d'eau-de-vie et de vin. A son retour, il était frais comme une rose."
(325).

Man often wants to share the purity that he discovers in nature with
his ideal woman. The author of the short story "Les Fraises" awakens on
a cool June morning, sees the skies swept clean by the storm of the preceding night and smells the good odor that emanates from the wet earth.
Drawn by these qualities of purity and freshness, he asks Ninon to
accompany him on a walk into the countryside.

This strong attraction toward purity in nature and the need to place the
ideal woman in the midst of nature frequently combine in Zola's works.
In a natural setting, the hero of *La Confession de Claude* conceives the
idea that the purity in nature may cleanse an impure woman. Claude
reminds his boyhood friends that on a certain June day, as they lay in the
grass by the river, he confided to them that his ideal woman should possess the pure, virginal qualities of nature: "...j'aurais voulu qu'elle naquît
pareille aux fleurs sauvages, en plein vent, en pleine rosée, qu'elle fût
plante des eaux, qu'un éternel courant lavât son cœur et sa chair. Je vous
jurais de n'aimer qu'une vierge, une vierge enfant, plus blanche que la
neige, plus limpide que l'eau de source, plus profonde et plus immense en
pureté que le ciel et la mer." (66-67) Thus the presence of nature incites a
thirst for purity and virginity, qualities essential, consequently, to his
image of the ideal woman. But Laurence, the prostitute with whom
Claude falls in love, is certainly not the girl of his dreams. Claude deplores
the fact that a man must often waste time with such fallen women before
finding the virginal woman whom he marries and asks: "Que ne m'atten-
dais-tu là-bas, dans les blés fleuris?" (24)

Yet Claude, unable to find that woman, trusts that nature can purify
Laurence. On the first day of spring he takes his jaded mistress on a long
country walk. Suddenly coming into a valley bursting with early spring,
Laurence leaves Claude's arm to run joyfully and freely on the grass (81).
This contact with nature elicits a spontaneity and wholesomeness in
Laurence, who recaptures

... ses quinze ans au sein de cette campagne qui n'avait pas quinze jours. La
jeune verdure rafraîchissait son sang, les jeunes rayons échauffaient son cœur,
rougissaient ses joues. Tout son être s'éveillait dans cet éveil de la terre; comme
la terre, elle redevenait vierge, la saison étant douce.
    Laurence courait follement, souple et forte, emportée par la vie nouvelle qui

chantait en son être.... Sa face entière s'était animée, les traits détendus, assouplis, avaient une bonne expression de joie. Le rire était franc, la voix sonore, le geste caressant. (82)

Nature, in turn, benefits by the presence of this exuberant being in its midst: "...le printemps avait plus de clarté, plus de vie, depuis que cette enfant blanche riait dans la verdure." (83)

The heroine of *Madeleine Férat*, who had a lover before she met Guillaume, undergoes a similar transformation. After walking for some time under a hot sun, she and Guillaume come into a cool shady area where her spontaneous, childlike reactions parallel those of Laurence. Madeleine, too, suddenly leaves her escort's arm and "se mit à courir comme un jeune chien pris de folie joyeuse. Toute sa puérilité se réveillait en elle, elle redevenait petite fille dans l'ombre fraîche, dans le silence frissonnant des arbres. ...les grâces enfantines de ses joues et de ses lèvres adoucissaient les lignes dures de son front." (11) Later Madeleine rents a country cottage in the vicinity of La Noiraude which Guillaume has occupied since his father's death. This is Madeleine's first sustained contact with life in the country: each day Guillaume is surprised by her growing beauty and blossoming health.

La campagne en faisait véritablement une autre femme. Elle paraissait avoir grandi encore.... Tout son être prenait des attitudes d'une vigueur superbe.

Elle avait retrouvé ses volontés, elle vivait sans secousse, obéissant à la simplicité naïve de son être. (100)

Daniel of *Le Vœu d'une morte* relies upon the landscape of Mesnil-Rouge to purify Jeanne of her spoiled city behavior. Awakening on the first morning of her stay at the Telliers' summer estate, she is moved to tears by the beauty of the serene landscape and runs outside. "Dans les fraîcheurs calmes de la jeune saison, elle retrouva subitement ses gaîtés, ses tranquillités de pensionnaire." (95) It is as though she were once again the small child laughing and running breathlessly about the trees in the convent playground before her exuberance was stifled by the conventions imposed by the salons. "Cette montée de sève n'était d'ailleurs encore que physique, car elle n'entendait pas son cœur battre dans cette sérénité des champs; et elle s'abandonnait simplement à la vie ardente qui brûlait en elle." (95)

Regained youth and purification of being are maintained only as long as the heroine — Laurence in *La Confession*, Jeanne of *Le Vœu*, and also Zola's Nana — remains in direct contact with nature.

The novelistic device of placing the purifying interlude in the country for Florent in the middle of *Le Ventre de Paris* is repeated in *Nana* for the heroine, thereby relieving tension for both protagonist and reader. Nana, a prostitute, like Laurence in *La Confession*, becomes virginal in natural surroundings. In its positive aspects her recaptured youth far surpasses her own childhood and youth in Paris, described in *L'Assommoir*.

Shortly after her arrival at Mignotte, the country property that Steiner purchased for her, Nana quickly inspects the house, looks out from the attic, and is enchanted by the immense horizon suffused in the gray mists of approaching rain. Upon spotting the vegetable garden below, she is so overjoyed that she collides with the maid in her dash down the stairs. She exclaims gleefully over cabbages, lettuces, spinach, artichokes, and other vegetables in the garden. By now the rain is falling in torrents, yet Nana is unperturbed by the scant protection her silken parasol offers. The down-pour does not dampen her enthusiasm in the least as she examines each fruit tree and vegetable. Dusk falls fast as the drenching rain becomes heavier, forcing Nana to feel the plants separately with her fingers. "Tout à coup, dans le crépuscule, elle distingua des fraises. Alors, son enfance éclata." (163) She shouts for Zoé to bring a plate and help her pick some of the strawberries. In her excitement she has let go of the parasol and now receives the full force of the driving rain in her face.

In the succeeding days she is like a blushing fifteen-year old virgin ashamed by new desires, a novel and fresh experience for Nana. "La campagne la trempait de tendresse.... Elle était ramenée aux sensations neuves d'une gamine." (172) For hours at a stretch she gazes sentimentally at the moon, and she takes moonlit walks under the trees with Georges.

Physical rejuvenation and childlike innocence may also be effected for either man or woman by the waters of a river. He who plunges into a river may find himself in a fountain of youth. The rejuvenating power of water upon the bather is noted in one of the "Souvenirs". As the author passes by one of the public baths in the Seine, the loud shouting of the playful bathers reminds him of a school recess. "L'homme redevient enfant, dans l'eau pure." (CN 387) In *L'Œuvre* Claude Lantier and Pierre Sandoz recall their boyhood days of swimming in the Viorne: "Ce ruis-sellement d'eau pure qui les trempait au grand soleil, prolongeait leur enfance, leur donnait des rires frais de galopins échappés." (38) The very coldness of the water becomes a morally cleansing agent in *La Fortune des Rougon*. Miette asks Silvère to teach her to swim; but being bashfully perturbed as to how to hold her in the water during her first lessons, he does not acquiesce immediately. The chill of the waters of the Viorne quickly washes away any apprehensions of anticipated shame: "Le froid du bain les mettait dans une pureté de cristal.... Silvère, après les premiers bains se reprocha secrètement d'avoir rêvé le mal." (221)

That the cold of rain and wind can purify, too, is a pleasurable experience for the acutely sensitive hero of *La Confession de Claude*. As Claude and Laurence leave a stuffy Parisian dance hall, an icy wind strikes them in the face. In contrast to Laurence who merely shivers in the cold, Claude experiences "une sensation délicieuse. Je me suis senti renaître au bien, à la vie libre et énergique; l'ivresse s'est dissipée, et sous la pluie fine de décembre, j'ai eu un instant d'ineffable volupté, jetant là tous les dégoûts de cette nuit brûlante. ... j'aurais voulu m'en aller par les rues, laissant l'eau glacée me pénétrer et renouveler mon être." (47)

Although *renaître* here simply signifies a renewal of energy, in the passages that follow the verb means to be reborn in a more total and more literal sense.

Zola's conception of rebirth stems from an actual experience recorded in the entries of his autobiographical "Le Printemps — journal d'un convalescent". As the sunrays first warm the hands of the convalescing Zola, he manifests a desire to live. And, when the sunshine floods the bed, he feels his body slowly come to life (LFAM 427). Later he sits before the window; and while the sun slowly approaches the horizon, the warm beams penetrate his flesh to warm his blood and to give vital sustenance to his entire being. But when the sun, upon which he is totally dependent now, sinks behind the horizon, he fears for his very life:

Il me semblait que je vivais de ses clartés, que mon corps faisait partie de sa lumière et de sa chaleur. Il était entré dans ma poitrine, il avait pris la place de mon cœur, il battait en moi et me donnait le souffle.

Comme le soleil disparaissait derrière les collines, une épouvante terrible m'a pris. Le soleil s'en allait, mon cœur s'en allait dans la nuit. J'ai tendu les mains vers l'astre pour retenir mon cœur qui s'arrachait de ma poitrine et qui partait avec le dernier rayon. Il ferait noir bientôt, je serais mort. (LFAM 428-429)

Man's rebirth in a natural environment develops into a central theme in the earlier phases of the hero's convalescence in *La Faute de l'abbé Mouret*. But before examining that experience and its preceding gestation period, it is significant to observe the relationship between nature and Serge Mouret, both as seminarist and priest.

During the five years of preparation for the priesthood, Serge and his fellow seminarists usually gathered on Thursday afternoons in a green meadow near the Viorne river. There, beneath the willows, they sat in groups reciting and studying, completely oblivious to the nature about them. The young man's apathy toward nature is prolonged into priesthood, due in large part to the barren landscape that surrounds his parish.

But one morning as the Abbé Mouret stands outside his church and gazes dreamily at the landscape, the warm sunshine relaxes him so gradually that he slips into a lizard-like lethargy and mistakes his physical well-being for a spiritual one. Later, while driving away from a house call that Dr. Pascal and he pay upon Jeanbernat, keeper of the Paradou, the priest is disturbed by the voluptuous shadows of the trees along the periphery of the vast park. He feels uneasy until he finds himself once again under the blinding sun and among the stony fields, surroundings that conform more to the desert landscape that his ascetic self seeks. "Le long du chemin creux, les arbres avaient laissé tomber sur sa nuque des fraîcheurs inquiétantes, que maintenant le soleil ardent séchait. Les maigres amandiers, les blés pauvres, les vignes infirmes, aux deux bords de la route, l'apaisaient, le tiraient du trouble où l'avaient jeté les souffles trop gras du Paradou." (67).

When Abbé Mouret becomes very ill, Pascal places the delirious priest in the care of Albine, Jeanbernat's niece. When the first crisis is past, Albine tries to convince Serge that what he needs now in order to get well are trees and coolness, not the rocky, burnt terrain which suited him in the past. Yet a single swaying tree branch casting its shadow on one window disquiets him, for it portends the imminent presence of the entire forest just beyond. Fearing the sight of this branch in all its raw, palpitating life, he refuses to have the curtains drawn aside.

On the next day a downpour admits only a pallid gray light past the curtains, depressing Serge. Slightly delirious, he declares sobbingly that the sun is dead and that he can hear all of nature bereaving that death. He empathizes with the buried seeds in their nightmarish upward struggle through the resistant soil to reach light, and he cries out desperately for spring to cure both him and the earth, made sick by winter.

Hypersensitive to each change in the nasty weather of the succeeding days, Serge insists that the shutters be kept closed and the lamp lit: "A certaines heures de nuages d'encre, lorsque les arbres tordus craquaient, que la terre laissait traîner ses herbes sous l'averse, comme des cheveux de noyée, il perdait jusqu'au souffle, il trépassait, battu lui-même par l'ouragan. Puis, à la première éclaircie, au moindre coin de bleu, entre deux nuées, il respirait, il goûtait l'apaisement des feuillages essuyés, des sentiers blanchissants, des champs buvant leur dernière gorgée d'eau." (148).

His empathy with the earth and its vegetation has also made Serge completely dependent upon the regenerative powers of the sun. When the simple presence of Albine's hand upon his cheek loses its efficacy to soothe him, Albine, too, strongly implores the sun to return. "Elle avait besoin de la complicité du printemps." (148) One morning Serge senses the return of the sun and tells Albine to open the shutters, but not the curtains. He is excited now by the sight of the swaying shadow of the branch which announces the revival of all life outside. Fearful that his health is still too delicate for exposure to the vitality of nature throbbing beyond the window, he postpones for two days drawing aside the curtains. "Derrière ce voile, derrière ce rêve attendri de la vie puissante du dehors, il écoutait monter le printemps. Et même il étouffait un peu, par moments, lorsque l'afflux du sang nouveau de la terre, malgré l'obstacle des rideaux, arrivait à lui trop rudement." (152)

Then one morning Albine pulls aside the curtains to let in the sunlight. In a short time Serge merges his identity with the pure blue sky extending into infinity; "et c'était déjà là un jet trop fort pour ses délicatesses de malade.... Il naissait. Il poussait de petits cris involontaires, noyé de clarté, battu par des vagues d'air chaud, sentant couler en lui tout un engouffrement de vie." (152)

In fact, the imagery of Serge's rebirth into the world of nature follows and translates the actual birth experiences of a newborn child. Within a womb-like enclosure of the shuttered room, a fetal Serge shared with agony in the subterranean struggle of the germinating seeds toward light and life outside. The final days of inclement weather endured by the hypersensitive Serge are like the pains of labor that precede childbirth, fully as traumatic to the prenatal being as to the mother. The 'veil' of the window curtains may then be compared to a membrane of the fetal sac that separates the expectant newborn from the independent energies of life beyond. Just prior to his exit from the womb, he suffered a slight spell of suffocation because of "the afflux of fresh blood from the earth". Serge is, in essence, reborn of Mother Nature.

Following his rebirth, Serge seems to derive vital sustenance directly from the sun. His subsequent renewal of strength incites a craving to encounter increasingly stronger physical sensations. He now longs for clouds to break up the monotonous purity of the blue sky and for the branch of the tree to grow and spread out before his eyes. On his first venture outdoors, Serge thrills to the continuing renascent processes that activate his whole being, as the phenomena of nature awaken each of his senses in rapid succession (164-165).

Florent of *Le Ventre de Paris* also experiences the sensation of rebirth in the presence of nature during his enjoyable day of respite from Les Halles at Mme François' farm. Again man is like an organism born not of woman but of Mother Nature from whom he derives, in plant-like dependence, his sustenance. Earth and air are his food for survival. Florent's subsequent return to Paris and to Les Halles, a severance from the source of vitality, parallels the diary entry in which the convalescent Zola describes his anguish at feeling his life ebb with the sinking sun before re-entry into his nightmare of a living death.

While Claude sketches the barn and Mme François prepares an omelet, Florent walks about the vegetable garden. "Il était profondément heureux de la paix et de la propreté de la terre.... Alors, les Halles qu'il avait laissées le matin, lui parurent un vaste ossuaire, un lieu de mort où ne traînait que le cadavre des êtres, un charnier de puanteur et de décomposition.... Le tapage, l'humidité nauséabonde du pavillon de la marée s'en allaient de lui; il renaissait à l'air pur. Claude avait raison, tout agonisait aux Halles. La terre était sa vie, l'éternel berceau, la santé du monde." (220) Mme François remarks that he looks ten years younger. Sitting on the ground near some fruit trees in the garden, Florent feels himself "renaissant dans la sève de la campagne, pareil à ce chou que Claude prétendait avoir vu pousser plus de dix fois" (221). And as he walks back to Paris with Claude, Florent remains silent, "assombri déjà, se disant qu'il laissait sa santé derrière lui" (221). As the setting sun projects the long, thin shadows of the two men upon the Arc de Triomphe, Florent senses his entrapment into the web of Paris. Night falls as he reaches Les Halles. "Il baissa la tête, en rentrant dans son cauchemar de nourritures gigantesques, avec le souvenir doux et triste de cette journée de santé claire, toute parfumée de thym." (224)

Rebirth for Laurent, of *Thérère Raquin*, contains only a subliminal hint of bodily resurrection. In his case, the stress is on simple revitalization. Spontaneous sensuous responses to spring weather permit him temporary escape from a conscience plagued for having drowned Camille. When daylight dissipates the terror that he shares nightly with Thérèse in fearful anticipation of Camille's apparition, Laurent strolls leisurely to his place of work, feeling the arrival of spring: "Laurent se sentait renaître dans l'air frais; il respirait largement ces souffles de vie jeune qui descendent des cieux d'avril et de mai; il cherchait le soleil, s'arrêtait pour regarder les reflets d'argent qui moiraient la Seine..., jouissait par tous ses sens de la matinée claire et heureuse." (159) For one whose sensuousness remains at an animal-like level of passive enjoyment, 'rebirth' primarily means renewed vigor, usually of brief duration. In this instance, physical purification is accompanied by mental pacification.

Occasionally the processes of purification and pacification blend, but most often they operate separately.

Earlier in the novel, varying degrees of cold exert a calming effect upon the troubled mind of Laurent. The briskness of midnight air momentarily dispels from his consciousness the persistent remembrance of the murder that he committed some hours previously (78). The soothing effect of cold air continues to be efficacious after his marriage with Camille's widow. The icy chill of January night winds occasionally admitted into the room tranquilizes his fear that the dead man's ghost might appear to haunt him and his bride during their frightful nightlong vigils.

The cold air of dawn, in *Madeleine Férat*, scatters the fearsome visions of an excessively lascivious wife which were tormenting Guillaume throughout the long, stormy night after he learned of Madeleine's former liaison with Jacques (167). The frigidity of the following wintry night, through which Guillaume flees with his wife in an open-air carriage, numbs his sorely troubled mind (182).

More clement weather can also be a sedative. The welcome cool of an evening breeze abates the ardent affection, feverishly intensified by the daytime heat, of the young lovers in the short story "Naïs Micoulin" (CN I 95). The coolness of sea breezes sometimes eases the sorrow of Blanche, who is closely guarded from seeing her lover, in *Les Mystères de Marseille*. Mild weather disperses anxiety for Count Muffat, in *Nana*. With tangible proof of his wife's infidelity, he plots vengeance throughout a long night; but on going outside, his train of thought is dissipated by the mildness of the beautiful June morning (358-359). In *La Bête humaine* the extraordinary mildness of one warm June night so assuages Jacques' remorse for having murdered his mistress Séverine, he opens the throttle on the new train engine, previously conducted with great caution, to allow it to breathe as freely as he does (339). It is the calmness and immensity of a dark starless sky that relaxes another murderer in the same novel. Often when the troubled Roubaud, the deputy stationmaster, has difficulty in napping in his office after midnight, he walks about the railroad yards until dawn. "Le vaste ciel noir, la paix souveraine de la nuit finissait par calmer sa fièvre." (169)

The immensity of other natural phenomena as well conduce strongly to the pacification of man. As the great pacifier, the immense sea lulls the sick at heart and the sick in body until health is recovered. Through a multiple appeal to the senses, the sea pacifies Blanche in *Les Mystères de Marseille*, whom her father holds as a virtual prisoner during her pregnancy, in a small house overlooking the sea near Saint-Henri. For days she listens to, and is soothed by, the steady rhythmic sounds of the lapping waves; the "gentle and monotonous immensity" of the sea further relaxes her troubled spirit (207). The long emotional crisis brought about by her forced separation from Philippe, and the severe physical strain she suffered in giving birth to their son result in a "fever" that almost proves fatal to Blanche. In spite of her wish to die, she gradually regains her strength; "les souffles âpres et sains de la mer qui entraient librement par ses fenêtres, l'obligèrent à vivre" (315). She gazes often and long from her window at the infinite sea. At this point, the author interjects a personal judgment: "Tous les malades devraient aller se guérir au bord des nappes bleues de la Méditerranée, car la vue de cette immensité calme a je ne sais quelle majesté tranquille qui apaise les douleurs." (316)

Perhaps some light can be shed upon this "je ne sais quoi" in another seaside scene of convalescence in Le Vœu d'une morte. On the eve of Jeanne's marriage to Lorin, Daniel falls ill, victim of a lengthy, burning fever. After the marriage, Daniel flees to the seashore at Saint-Henri where he had once spent a peaceful existence and now rents a room facing the sea. Its broad blue expanse calms him, and he gradually regains his strength.

Le bruit des flots avait comme un écho dans sa poitrine, et il laissait bercer ses pensées. Il s'asseyait sur une pointe de rocher, tournant le dos aux vivants, s'absorbant dans l'infini. Et il était seulement heureux lorsque les vagues avaient endormi sa mémoire et qu'il était là, inerte, en extase, dormant les yeux ouverts.

Alors, une étrange hallucination le hantait. Il croyait être le jouet des flots, il s'imaginait que la mer était montée le prendre et qu'elle le balançait maintenant avec douceur. (107-08)

Thus, a return to a previously peaceful existence, reinforced by the combined imagery of being absorbed into the infinity of nature and rocked tenderly in a state of suspension by a maternal sea, illustrates again a repressed wish on the part of another Zola character to return to the womb and a prenatal existence. Moreover, it should be noted that the semi-conscious Daniel has turned his back upon the source of his anxieties and that his seated posture on a rock may indeed resemble the fetal position.

But the repressed desire to return to the womb fuses only feebly with a strong death wish and the expressed psychopathic desire for loss of identity when he seeks solace from the sea on a second occasion, namely, after bringing the widowed Jeanne and his good friend Georges together. Too weak to leave his room, he spends his time looking avec passion at the sea and in "losing himself" in the "purity" of the blue double infinities of water and sky, "dans ce large trou d'azur qui lui semblait s'ouvrir sur l'autre vie. Tout au fond, il voyait parfois des lueurs aveuglantes, où il aurait voulu s'anéantir." (132)

Like the sea, certain landscapes have a tranquilizing effect upon Zola's characters. In fact, in *Madeleine Férat*, a nocturnal landscape practically lulls Guillaume into a state of numbness that exposes for him a repressed wish for the repose of death. In an open gig, he and Madeleine flee by night across a countryside glazed in ice. "Ces roideurs des horizons morts lui faisaient rêver alors les douceurs d'une immobilité éternelle." (182) The above landscape, however, is exceptional. Broad, calm lines, however, normally characterize the landscapes that pacify, like the one surrounding Mesnil-Rouge, the Telliers' summer estate, in *Le Vœu d'une morte*: "Contrée douce et consolante, horizons d'une largeur sereine, dans lesquels le cœur s'apaisait." (94-95)

The pacifying qualities of immensity, majesty, and serenity combine also in certain growths of trees. In "Le Bois", one of the "Esquisses parisiennes", Zola remembers how much he enjoyed strolling in the Verrières woods. There, lanes led into vast leaf-walled halls lined by tall, stately column-like trees, whose leafy domes suggest the interior of a church nave, one conducive to meditation (CN I 66). The quasi-religious communion deepens in "La Rivière", another of the "Esquisses", when the spectator views stately trees that double their height by reflecting their image upon the waters. The authors and some friends would row a boat for a while up the Seine and then let it float slowly down the river again. They would converse until they came in sight of three islands, studded with tall green trees, their lengths extended once again upon the mirrored surface, and then

un recueillement invincible nous envahissait peu à peu.
... Une sérénité, une majesté, venaient de ces deux azurs, le ciel et le fleuve, où le sommeil des arbres était si pur. Le soir, surtout, quand pas une feuille ne remuait, quand la nappe d'eau prenait le poli bleuâtre de l'acier, le spectacle s'élargissait encore et faisait rêver d'infini. (CN I 75)

On the one hand, the serene quiescence and stillness of nature, the "so pure sleep" and dreaming of infinity can appeal to a repressed wish for the repose of death; on the other, meditation, peaceful to be sure, is nevertheless a mental activity.

Once nature has pacified man, its next step may be to inspire in him optimistic expectations.

Calm nature infuses "immense hope" in Daniel of *Le Vœu d'une morte* when he indulges in the serenity of the river islands (97). On the occasions that Jeanne accompanies him there before dusk, his hope of permanently converting her character extends into the twilight hour. They let the boat carry them gently downstream among the islands, gambol childishly ashore for a while, and afterwards row slowly homeward in the pale twilight, allowing their boat to linger leisurely in cool, shadowy channels. Peace permeates Daniel's entire being, so much so that he mistakingly assumes that the tenderness in nature has equally suffused Jeanne and penetrated deeply for permanent absorption into her character. But when Lorin, whose mere presence causes Jeanne to lapse into her displeasing urbane behavior, comes to ask the Telliers for her hand in marriage, Daniel realizes "qu'il s'était trop oublié dans la volupté douce du Mesnil-Rouge" (104).

In *Madeleine Férat* the warmth of the great outdoors disperses the defenses that Guillaume and Madeleine have built up against each other, for they were embarrassed and awkward with their friendship, so recent and so quick: "Leur esprit s'était détendu aux tiédeurs du soleil, dans l'air libre qui leur soufflait à la face des bouffées âpres et chaudes. ...la campagne les pénétrait d'un tel bien-être qu'ils ne songeaient plus à s'observer ni à se défendre l'un contre l'autre." (10-11) After they spend the night together, a sunny morning landscape mellows Madeleine even more as she daydreams before the open window, "le visage détendu par des pensées plus calmes, par des espérances lointaines" (23).

The sun in particular reduces the tensions in man, prepares him to receive hope. Fleeing by night, the young Philippe Cayol and Blanche de Cazalis of *Les Mystères de Marseille* are terrified by the nocturnal awesomeness of the gorge-gutted, rock-hilled terrain from Marseille to Aix; but dawn dissolves that living nightmare for them, and hope resurges with the morning sun (31). Just before the conclusion of *La Terre*, Jean is deserted by his fellow mourners, attracted to a fire nearby. He stands alone in the cemetery gazing down at the freshly covered graves of his wife and old Fouan. His bad humor gradually evaporates beneath a warm sun: "Ses colères du matin, son dégoût des gens et des choses s'en allaient, dans un profond apaisement. Il se sentait, malgré lui, peut-être à cause du tiède soleil, envahi de douceur et d'espoir." (515)

This combination of calm and hope engendered by a warm sun is exploited at greater length in the character of Mme Caroline in *L'Argent*. In his outline for the novel, Zola assigns a symbolic role of hope to her: "*Elle est l'espoir*.... Dès qu'elle est dans la rue, au soleil, elle se reprend à aimer, à espérer, à être heureuse." (442) Mme Caroline tells Saccard that whenever she goes out into the street in the sunshine following any moral or emotional crisis, hope springs anew for her (75). The salient example of this phenomenon appears at the end of the novel, just as the sun inspires renewed hope in Jean toward the conclusion of *La Terre*, cited in the preceding paragraph. Mme Caroline agonizes over each victim's death or ruin contributed to the crash of stocks in the Banque Universelle. After leaving the dead Sigismond in the arms of his brother, she descends to the street and out into the exceptionally mild air. "Cet avril, si charmant d'une nouvelle jeunesse, était comme une caresse à tout son être physique, jusqu'au cœur. Elle respira fortement, soulagée, plus heureuse déjà, avec la sensation de l'invincible espoir qui revenait et grandissait." (425) Heady scents of violets and stock from a flower cart elicit throughout her being a continually swelling wave of joy that the conscience-stricken woman tries in vain to quell. In view of the recent human tragedies, she feels she should be mournful, not cheerful; but

... le bouillonnement de sève devenait plus impérieux, la source de vie débordait, écartait les obstacles pour couler librement, en rejetant les épaves aux deux bords, claire et triomphante sous le soleil.

Dès ce moment, vaincue, Mme Caroline dut s'abandonner à la force irrésistible du continuel rajeunissement. ... elle venait de toucher le fond du désespoir, et voici que l'espoir ressuscitait de nouveau brisé, ensanglanté, mais vivace quand même, plus large de minute en minute. Certes, aucune illusion ne lui restait, la vie était décidément injuste et ignoble, comme la nature.... Puis, lorsqu'elle tourna dans la rue de la Chausseé-d'Antin, elle ne raisonna même plus; la philosophe, en elle, la savante et la lettrée abdiquait, fatiguée de l'inutile recherche des causes; elle n'était plus qu'une créature heureuse du beau ciel et de l'air doux, goûtant l'unique jouissance de se bien porter... Ah! la joie d'être, est-ce qu'au fond il en existe une autre? La vie telle qu'elle est, dans sa force, si abominable qu'elle soit, avec son éternel espoir! (426-427)

Except for these latter examples where pacification engenders optimism, nature generally stops short of inspiring hope and only purifies man of a disturbing emotion. As the great sedative, nature assuages man's painful tensions, soothes his immediate anxieties.

Through purification and pacification, man retreats consciously and unconsciously into his past. By renewing contact with the sunny nature that he knew as a child or as an adolescent, man recaptures the wholesomeness and exuberant freedom of his youth. Both Zola and his autobiographical hero of *La Confession de Claude* had nurtured visions of loving virgin girls in a natural setting; but when their first important romance involved instead a prostitute,[1] the author and Claude each

---

[1] Regarding the relationship of Zola and the prostitute Berthe, see Henri Guillemin, *Zola légende ou vérité?* (Paris, 1960), pp. 14-20.

probed the possibility then of whether nature, as they intimately knew it, could return a state of virginity to the fallen woman. But the transferability of purity in nature to woman did not meet their expectations. Suffused by the purity of nature, the impure woman generally responded by acts of simple physical rejuvenation; or if there appeared to be any actual transfusion of purity, it was of short duration, only effective for as long as she remained in direct contact with nature. Perhaps Zola renews here the age-old concept that woman is basically impure. Disillusionment ensues when man sees that nature is incapable of rendering a total and permanent cleansing and purification of her body and spirit. Then he escapes alone into nature for self-rejuvenation and solace. Thus, psychic energy is shunted from his beloved to some phenomenon of nature, from objective reality to subjective imagery. This object cathexis gratifies the disillusioned lover.

Sigmund Freud, in *Beyond the Pleasure Principle*, argued that "the aim of all life is death".[2] By this, he means that organic matter strives constantly to return to the inanimate, quiescent state from which it was initially disturbed. This instinct is "the expression of inertia inherent in organic life."[3] Man comes from a state of equilibrium in the womb into a world where tensions beset him constantly. Sometimes he can resolve those that lie in the pit of the unconscious through the dream process. At times he can bring them into equilibrium through object cathexis. The greater the tensions, the further man seeks to regress in his unconsciousness, whether to the pleasant security of prenatal suspension or to the ultimate repose in death.

Thus, search for purification thrusts man further and further into his past, beyond regained youth and childhood, to a concept of rebirth. Reborn man is rendered pure again and often finds himself in a better world, a world in its infancy and innocence. But often search for the lost paradise embraces repressed wishes to plunge still deeper into his past, and his need for pacification dominates his need for purification. In his regression toward passivity and voids of non-being, man is purged of life itself.

Purification and pacification represent in part evasive flights into the past, whether a short return to a state of being preceding anxiety, or a longer return to the innocence and vigor of past youth and childhood, the purity of rebirth, the passive existence in the womb, or total nothingness.

---

[2] Sigmund Freud, *Beyond the Pleasure Principle*, Standard edition, Vol. XVIII (London: Hogarth Press, 1955), p. 38.
[3] *Beyond the Pleasure Principle*, p. 36.

IV

A SOURCE OF ANXIETY

Au dedans de moi le soir tombe.
O terre, dont la brume efface les sommets,
Suis-je le spectre, et toi la tombe?
Hugo

A serene nature suppresses immediate anxieties from the preconscious of man, sublimates the loss of a lover's illusion into object cathexis, or represses the wish to return to the womb or to die. Conversely, an agitated nature bares for man an underlying, disturbing element or causes a death wish to rise from the unconscious id to the surface of consciousness. Passive physical or psychical contentment cedes to conscious emotional agitation. The released death wish turns into fear of death or desire for self-destruction.

Repressed wishes for a return to the womb, for death, and for oblivion merge in curious fashion as they infiltrate the consciousness of some of Zola's characters. Selections from a short story and a novel offer a striking illustration of how dusk and the dying day affect them. "Morale", the last section of the "Aventures du grand Sidoine et du petit Médéric", opens with a description of the fleeting reign of twilight over the countryside: "La terre, voilée d'une ombre douce, sommeillait déjà à demi, rêveuse et mélancolique. Au-dessus des horizons s'étendait un ciel blanc, sans transparence." (CN 261) Why does the author attribute melancholy to this time of day?

Il est une heure, chaque soir, d'une profonde tristesse; la nuit n'est pas encore, la lumière s'éteint lentement, comme à regret; et l'homme, dans cet adieu, se sent au cœur une vague inquiétude, un besoin immense d'espérance et de foi. Les premiers rayons du matin mettent des chansons sur les lèvres; les derniers rayons du soir mettent des larmes dans les yeux. Est-ce la pensée désolante du labeur sans cesse repris, sans cesse abandonné, l'âpre désir mêlé d'effroi d'un repos éternel? Est-ce la ressemblance de toutes choses humaines avec cette lente agonie de la lumière et du bruit? (CN 261)

And in this moment of "l'effacement de la terre et du ciel" (CN 261), man senses with anguish his mortal condition, his eventual oblivion.

A counterpart to this passage occurs in the description of that hour of dusk just preceding the tragic conclusion of *Madeleine Férat*. The two texts, similar in imagery, illuminate each other. At the same time, they shed more light upon the strange mixture formed when repressed wishes for a state of quiet suspension and for nothingness begin to penetrate the consciousness and are agitated by anxiety.

Madeleine, seduced in Paris by her former lover, decides to commit suicide and returns home to explain this decision to her husband. Near Véteuil she gets off the stage coach and heads toward La Noiraude. "Le crépuscule tombait, d'une douceur exquise. Les horizons tremblants s'évanouissaient dans la nuit. Les champs devenaient noirs sous le ciel laiteux, frissonnants d'un bruit de prières et de chansons mourantes, qui traînaient au fond du jour agonisant." (280) A quality of softness and gentleness characterizes the descriptions quoted from both "Morale" and *Madeleine Férat*. Also the white translucency of the sky described in the first text is qualified in the second as "milky". In both examples the veiled evanescence of the vision educes melancholy. For a psychoanalyst this combined imagery may contain an undefined longing for the beholder to return to the womb, a return impossible to attain. And so, another dimension is insinuated as the white translucent or milky sky embraces death with its shroud. There is nothing contradictory here in the formation of the two repressed wishes, for both are devices to reduce tension and seek a state of equilibrium.

The 'agonizing' aspect is further heightened when the scene switches to Guillaume who, caught up in that same dusk, consciously seeks to fulfill a wish for death and nihility. Upon his return from Paris, he learned that his little daughter had died earlier in the afternoon. Grief-stricken, he walks about the park until dusk. "Lorsque le crépuscule tomba comme une cendre fine, donnant à la campagne une teinte grise uniforme d'une mélancolie poignante, il se sentit pris d'un accablement sans bornes, il eut un désir âpre de s'enfouir dans quelque trou lugubre où il pourrait contenter le besoin d'anéantissement qu'il éprouvait." (287) The dualism of the womb and the grave has resolved itself: the death wish clearly dominates now. The descending gray ashes of dusk darken the lactescence of twilight and presage the extinction of light and life. Cast into a state of complete dejection by the melancholy and agonizing aspects of nature, the anguished hero seeks the nothingness of death.

Dusk easily draws forth anxiety from the preconscious and the unconscious of man. In *La Fortune des Rougon*, on the day following the insurgents' night march through Plassans, an undefined fear settles with falling dusk upon the town, and Pierre Rougon shudders, caught in "this current of terror" (268). After the murder of Camille, both the heroine of *Thérèse Raquin* and Laurent, her second husband, relax during the daylight hours; but each dusk renews their nervousness and terror (163). Twilight seeps into the studio as Claude and Sandoz of *L'Œuvre* discuss the vanity of glory; and, "penetrated by the melancholy of dusk", Sandoz discloses his pessimistic thoughts about human suffering (285).

The series of cloudy, gloomy days that follow a few sunny hours stretch into an eternal, anguish-filled dusk for Zola in "Le Printemps — journal d'un convalescent". Through his feverish vision, the young author, a pained spectator, watches the funeral held by the natural forces for the sun. The obsequies are performed solemnly beneath the vast shroud of a translucent gray sky. "...je souffre dans cet air gris et humide que je respire avec effort et qui me glace la poitrine." (LFAM 429) The sky feels to him like a thick layer of black ashes, "un linceul qui recouvre le grand cadavre du soleil. Le vent souffle, et j'entends de brusques roulements de tambour, menant les funérailles célestes. ...ce rideau funèbre, toujours tiré devant moi, est à la longue plein d'épouvante.... Il me semble être en face du néant, éternellement morne, éternellement sombre." (LFAM 430) And as fever overtakes him again, he plummets, endlessly, into a dark nothingness. Winter continues; its somber gray skies do not vary. "Peu à peu, en face de l'air morne, une tristesse indicible s'est emparée de moi. J'ai eu, les yeux ouverts, des cauchemars d'enfant, des peurs soudaines et ridicules. Rien, pas une nuée ne passait dans le ciel noir, et mes regards, fixés anxieusement sur l'horizon, s'hallucinaient à chercher en vain un nuage, une teinte plus pâle qui annonçât le retour du soleil; je finissais par voir des ombres monstrueuses agitant leurs ailes et menaçant la terre." (LFAM 433) And unable to bear the view of this "sinister curtain" any longer, the author asks Françoise to close the shutters and light the lamp (LFAM 433).

The heroine of *L'Assommoir* is also confronted by a sinister curtain, but one more menacing to her person, for it threatens to enshroud her. Gnawing starvation doubles Gervaise's sensitivity to the biting cold of mid-January. The "bleak daylight made the marrow of her bones turn cold" (409). A snowstorm is imminent. She has a nightmare in which she dreams that the snow-burdened sky crushes down on her (411). Later when Gervaise finds her husband drinking in a tavern, his money gone, she becomes infuriated and decides to prostitute herself for money to buy food. While waiting for the cover of night before accosting some man, she walks aimlessly about the city. Her wanderings lead her into the affluent and spacious quarter of La Chaussée de Clignancourt where the Magenta and Ornano boulevards expose to view large stretches of sky. Although many people mill about her, Gervaise feels completely alone and lost. One of the elements contributing to this sentiment is "ce pan démesuré de ciel gris, tendu au-dessus d'un si vaste espace"; another is "cette sale couleur jaune des crépuscules parisiens, une couleur qui donne envie de mourir tout de suite" (424).

'Sinister', too, could define the curtain of twilight in *La Curée* that cloaks the latent depravity of the heroine and bares her frustration. The novel opens with a description of a sunset that, in an autumnal light gray sky, bathes the Bois de Boulogne in a pale reddish glow. Renée and her stepson Maxime lounge in one of the many carriages which proceed at a monotonous pace about the Bois. For no apparent reason, Renée confesses to Maxime that she is bored. However, it is the new broad vista that prompts her statement, for their carriage has brought them to that part of the Bois which opens out "en larges pelouses, en immenses tapis d'herbe, plantés çà et là d'un bouquet de grands arbres; les nappes vertes se suivaient, avec des ondulations légères, ...Renée regardait, les yeux fixes, comme si cet agrandissement de l'horizon, ces prairies molles, trempées par l'air du soir, lui eussent fait sentir plus vivement le vide de son être." (12)

When she speaks again of her boredom, Maxime protests that she possesses, and has done absolutely everything any woman could wish. But Renée counters that some desire still remains unfulfilled, though she cannot identify it. And she turns around to watch the landscape dissolve slowly into the "fine ashes" of falling dusk. Above the still lake, "le creux du ciel s'ouvrait, infini, plus profound et plus large. Ce grand morceau de ciel sur ce petit coin de nature, avait un frisson, une tristesse vague; et il tombait de ces hauteurs pâlissantes une telle mélancolie d'automne, une nuit si douce et si navrée, que le Bois, peu à peu enveloppé dans un linceul d'ombre, perdait ses grâces mondaines, agrandi, tout plein du charme puissant des forêts." (14-15) By now the dying embers of the sun glow in only one part of the immense gray sky. The fading landscape suggests a setting for the adulterous and incestuous loves of ancient gods, and Renée senses shameful desires arise within her. "Et, à mesure que la calèche s'éloignait, il lui semblait que le crépuscule emportait derrière elle, dans ses voiles tremblants, la terre du rêve, l'alcôve honteuse et surhumaine où elle eût enfin assouvi son cœur malade, sa chair lassée." (15)

Renée resumes the conversation, wondering whether she seeks at present the free bachelor existence of a Laure d'Aurigny or perhaps, preferably, something even more unusual. Maxime suggests a love of a criminal nature. She does not reply. "Elle était mollement envahie par l'ombre du crépuscule; tout ce que cette ombre contenait de tristesse, de discrète volupté, d'espoir inavoué, la pénétrait, la baignait dans une sorte d'air alangui et morbide." (17) The falling night, the constant rumbling and gentle rocking of the carriage diminishes her power of concentration. "Mille petits souffles lui passaient sur la chair: songeries inachevées, voluptés innomées, souhaits confus, tout ce qu'un retour de Bois, à l'heure où le ciel pâlit, peut mettre d'exquis et de monstrueux dans le cœur lassé d'une femme." (18)

The very immensity of a melancholy, crepuscular sky is primarily instrumental, then, in affecting the moods of the convalescent Zola, the victimized Gervaise, and the frustrated Renée. The immensity of a nocturnal sky increases thousandfold when the appearance of stars reveals the third dimension of depth. The immensity of a night sky, rather than a crepuscular one, will disturb the heroine of *Une Page d'amour*, for, unlike most of the characters in the preceding examples, she enjoys positively "le charme du crépuscule, l'effacement dernier des choses, l'assoupissement des bruis" (200). She has just opened wide the window at the close of a hot September day and looks out upon the darkening scene. Abbé Jouve joins her at the window. In silence they gaze upward at the countless stars that continue to emerge and extend the outer limits deeper and deeper into infinity. This spatial expansion evokes in Hélène "le sentiment poignant d'une immense douleur, d'un vide insondable qu'elle ne comblerait jamais" (203). Frightened by the limitless depths of the sky, Hélène turns her gaze downward upon the city, now engulfed in dark shadows. The priest notices that she is crying. "Le vaste horizon de Paris, au crépuscule, la touchait d'une profonde impression religieuse. La plaine semblait s'élargir…. Un besoin de foi, d'amour, d'anéantissement divin, lui donnait un grand frisson. Et c'était alors que le lever des étoiles la bouleversait d'une jouissance et d'une terreur sacrées." (203)

The priest asks her to confide in him. She replies that she was rarely inside a church during her childhood, but that she feels a strong need for faith now. Failing to encourage more intimate confidences, the priest tells Hélène that she must be in love. Hélène does not protest, but, in silence, watches the lights begin to appear here and there about the city. It is like the reflected rebirth of the starry night itself: "…les feux continuaient le ciel au-dessous de l'horizon, dans un prolongement de l'infini, comme si la terre eût disparu et qu'on eût aperçu de tous côtés la rondeur céleste. Et elle retrouvait là l'émotion qui l'avait brisée quelques minutes aupara-vant.... Paris, qui s'allumait, s'étendait, mélancolique et profond, appor-tant les songeries terrifiantes d'un firmament où pullulent les mondes." (204) The priest warns her that she is like so many women who mistake the God they seek in church for some man they love in this world. She confesses then that she is in love with Henri Deberle, a married man. The priest advises her to marry an honorable man, such as his own brother, Rambaud. Indicating the vast stretches of the nocturnal panorama with a broad sweep of his hand, he begs her not to refuse happiness and declares that her agitation disaccords with the beauty and peace of the night. But Hélène protests that he does not understand her, because it is precisely that nocturnal beauty which "agitates" her (209).

The illimitable vastness of a bright, starry night also overwhelms and forces down the gaze of the young lovers in "Naïs Micoulin": "Et le ciel, élargi au-dessus du chaos noir de l'horizon, était pour eux un grand charme, un charme qui les inquiétait et les faisait se serrer davantage.... Frémissant sous ces vastes espaces, ils baissaient la tête." (CN I 95)

The myriad of stars terrorize Lazare Chanteau of *La Joie de vivre*. One evening as he and the ten-year old Pauline Quenu lie stretched out on the sand beside the sea, Pauline comments on the beauty of the stars. Lazare, whose eyes disclose an "inner uneasiness", admits that he does not like to look at the stars because they frighten him. The sea seems to echo his despair as the ever expanding outer spaces exert their increasing weight upon him. "Sur l'immense horizon, noir maintenant, flambait la poussière volante des mondes. Et, dans cette plainte de la terre écrasée sous le nombre sans fin des étoiles" (46), Pauline hears Lazare sob; she asks if he is ill. He finally stammers out a wish to die.

For one who actually faces death, however, the reaction to a starry sky is quite the opposite. As Marie of *La Confession de Claude* lies dying, she gazes out at the stars on a warm night; and Claude reads into her expres-sion regret at having to depart from the vital forces of the universe (130).

Thus, cosmic agitation, when visible in a star-filled sky, arouses either a dormant feeling or quickens an already vibrant emotion in man. He relaxes only when the blackness of night hides the stars, as illustrated in our preceding chapter in which a starless sky calms the murderer Rou-baud of *La Bête humaine* (169).

The immensity of a landscape can depress or otherwise adversely affect man. Mme Tellier of *Le Voeu d'une morte* finds nature repulsive and does not enjoy her summers at Mesnil-Rouge, away from Paris. Gladly she welcomes the arrival of any visitor, for then she can entertain in the drawingroom. But should she, forgetting to draw the curtains, chance to look out, she becomes frightened by the perspective of the broad horizon: "...elle se sentait toute petite dans cette immensité, et son orgueil de femme en souffrait." (96)

The expansiveness of the flat plains of Beauce contributes to the deterioration of Abbé Madeline's health during the two and a half years that he ministers to the needs of his parishioners in *La Terre*. "La nostalgie, le regret désespéré de ses montagnes d'Auvergne l'avait rongé un peu chaque jour, en face de cette plate Beauce, dont le déroulement à l'infini noyait son cœur de tristesse." (458) These featureless plains stretching to infinity affect the native Beauceron differently: while the surveyor Grobois explains how Fouan's land might be divided among the old man's progeny, the interested parties assembled in the middle of the limitless, monotonous expanses have the 'dreaming' and 'reflective' traits of sailors accustomed to solitude and open spaces (42).

It is precisely this 'reflective' aspect engendered by an immense landscape which can separate a couple into two isolated beings. One October day Jean Macquart and Françoise Mouche converse as they walk along a country road. Suddenly aware of the endless fields that encompass them beneath the ashen sky, they lapse into silence, "comme envahis par la gravité réfléchie de cette Beauce, si triste et si féconde" (15).

The two young lovers in *La Fortune des Rougon* take a precautionary measure against another immense landscape. One wintry moonlit night Silvère and Miette walk along a road where extensive fields spread out on both sides of them. Since they do not walk separately but rather as one being enclosed in Miette's fur-lined cloak, they are not subject to "cet écrasement que les larges horizons indifférents font peser sur les tendresses humaines" (32). Protectively wrapped together in the security of a single cloak, they can enjoy the various aspects of these vast expanses as one would in looking out from the window of a house; and, thus, "cette vallée entière qui, en les charmant, n'était cependant pas assez forte pour se mettre entre leurs deux cœurs serrés l'un contre l'autre" (32).

However, the two principal protagonists of *Madeleine Férat* do not possess such a protective cloak. While climbing a hilly path Madeleine and Guillaume exchange smiles and loving glances. Guillaume is mustering courage to kiss her; but at the top of the hill an immense plateau fans out before them, and they no longer feel hidden from the rest of the world. "Bien que la campagne fût déserte, ils eurent peur de cette large étendue. Ils se séparèrent, inquiets, embarrassés de nouveau." (12-13)

An autumnal setting has much the same effect as does the broad horizon upon these two lovers. The arrival of autumn, which presages the inconvenience of clandestine meetings in winter cold, hastens Guillaume's decision to propose marriage to Madeleine. He wants La Source, their favorite natural scene, to serve as the setting for the proposal. However the desolate and melancholy autumn scene there silences for a while his wish to speak: "...les arbres étaient si nus, le ciel si triste, qu'il se taisait, frissonnant sous les premiers souffles de l'hiver." (102-103)

Wet and bleak wintry weather is also a great depressant for man. When Guillaume learns from Madeleine that Jacques, whom he had unexpectedly brought home as a house guest, was once her lover, they flee through the raging wind and driving rain of a pitch-black night to the cottage in which Madeleine lived before their marriage. But the wailing "death rattles" of the chill wind penetrate the walls of this once cozy cottage to further unnerve the already troubled couple within. Now that their love may be moribund, Madeleine, who formerly loved storms, has become as fearfully sensitive as Guillaume to this one. The storm, as though set loose by the furies, rages, and howls, while sheets of rain "battaient sur le toit un roulement sourd et continu de tambours menant des funérailles. Les époux souffraient des éclats de l'ouragan; chaque secousse, chaque lamentation les agitaient d'un malaise vague; des inquiétudes subites les prenaient." (159)

Dawn discloses a muddy landscape. The low overcast sky and the flat open countryside are cast in uniform grayness. The perspective nauseates the couple: "Le jour terne qui agonisait sur cette immensité boueuse, avait une clarté louche, sans reflet, dont la teinte sale faisait monter le dégoût à la gorge." (165) And shortly afterwards: "Cette heure trouble d'une matinée d'hiver est poignante pour les gens qui ont veillé toute la nuit. Guillaume regardait l'horizon sale avec un hébétement doulou-reux.... Elle laissa échapper un geste d'écœurement, en la voyant si fangeuse." (165-166) Dejected by the spectacle, they let the curtains fall back. Their flight to Paris is aborted when, at an inn enroute, Jacques chances to encounter Madeleine briefly in the very same room they had once shared as lovers. Later, she tells her husband of the memories immured in this room; and, more despondent than ever, they return to La Noiraude. The dismal winter scene there weighs even more heavily upon them as they, in turn, project their gloom upon it. They spend a funereal solitude in the huge black dining hall; "ils y vivaient dans un continuel frisson, attristés par le jour sale d'hiver, se croyant au fond d'une fosse. Ils se levaient parfois, allaient à la fenêtre, jetaient un coup d'œil désolé sur les arbres nus du parc, puis revenaient, avec des frémissements subits, présenter leurs mains froides à la flamme." (227)

The penetrating humidity and overcast skies of winter weigh heavily upon the hero of "Les Quatre journées de Jean Gourdon" in the final section, "Hiver". With the first thaw comes a disquieting, thick fog that cloaks the tragic events to follow. The bleak sky causes Jean to shudder: he will not, after all, work in the fields that day; "je ne sais rien de plus attristant que ces temps fades de dégel; je hais les brouillards dont l'humidité pèse aux épaules" (CN 460). The wintry cold and damp of Paris prompt a parallel response in "La Neige", one of the "Esquisses parisiennes", an echo of the author's own dejection when he looks out from his window at the typical gloom of a winter morning in Paris: "...rien n'est attristant comme la rue noire d'humidité et de froid. L'air sue un brouillard jaunâtre qui traîne lugubrement contre les murs." (CN I 44) The whiteness and purity of a fresh snowfall cheers the Parisians. But then the inevitable "frightful" thaw leaves in its muddy wake a Paris even more "dismal" than before the snow, as it soils and changes the "bridal gown" of the city into "rags which drag disgracefully on the paving-stones" (CN I 47).

The outskirts of a city are also repulsive tattered rags that have a disheartening effect upon man in *La Confession de Claude*. During their walk away from the city, Claude and Laurence wander onto the flat, treeless open country of the Montrouge zone lying at the periphery of the city. Its utter sordidness and huge man-wrought lacerations depress the couple: "Çà et là, le sol noir bâille affreusement, montrant, comme des entrailles ouvertes, d'anciennes carrières abandonnées, blafardes et profondes.... Tout est cru à l'œil, les terrains noirs, les pierres blanches, le ciel bleu. Le paysage entier, avec son aspect maladif, ses plans brusquement coupés, ses plaies béantes, a la tristesse indicible des contrées que la main de l'homme a déchirées." (80)

Claude deplores the desolation and bleakness of these man-mutilated expanses that lie on the outskirts of a city, because they contain neither the creations of its citizens nor "God's verdure or majesty" (80).

Zola is fully as disheartened and disgusted as his autobiographical Claude by the manner in which man has defaced, violated, mangled and butchered the belt of nature that encircles the city. He asserts his personal dislike for that no-man's land between a city proper and the country in "La Banlieue", one of the "Esquisses parisiennes":

Je ne connais rien de si laid ni de plus sinistre que cette première zone entourant Paris. Toute grande ville se fait ainsi une ceinture de ruines. A mesure que les pavés avancent, la campagne recule, et il y a, entre les rues qui finissent et l'herbe qui commence, une région ravagée, une nature massacrée dont les quartiers nouveaux n'ont pas encore caché les plaies.... Paris semble ainsi jeter continuellement son écume à ses bords.

On trouve là toute la saleté et tout le crime de la grande ville. L'ordure vient s'y mûrir au soleil. La misère y apporte sa vermine....

Certains coins sont surtout inquiétants. Je citerai la plaine de Montrouge, d'Arcueil à Vanves. Là s'ouvrent d'anciennes carrières, qui ont bouleversé le sol; et, au-dessus de la plaine nue, des treuils, des roues immenses se dressent sur l'horizon, avec des profils de gibets et de guillotines. Le sol est crayeux, la poussière a mangé l'herbe, on suit des routes défoncées, creusées d'ornières profondes, au milieu de précipices que les eaux de pluie changent en mares saumâtres. Je ne connais pas un horizon plus désolé, d'une mélancolie plus désespérée à l'heure où le soleil se couche, en allongeant les ombres grêles des grands treuils. (CN I 56-57)[1]

Although Zola's characters generally react in the same vein to the same phenomena of nature, a few, and within the same novels, do react in a radically different manner.

In *Le Vœu d'une morte*, the landscape surrounding the Telliers' summer estate rejuvenates Jeanne but repels Mme Tellier. For the latter the grass and plants stain her dresses, the sun burns her skin, the river is dirty, and the dead leaves under foot are frightening. With disgust and annoyance she watches Jeanne cavort about the grounds, and waspishly reminds her that such gambols do not become a well-bred Parisian girl. In time Jeanne acquires some of the older woman's skittish repugnance for nature. Before returning to the city, Daniel and Jeanne take a last walk on one of the islands in the Seine. The autumnal setting which enchants Daniel repulses Jeanne who remains silent. For her the reddened foliage is ugly (99).

In *La Conquête de Plassans*, the opposing reactions of Marthe and her daughter Désirée to the earth are more extreme. The mentally retarded, seventeen-year old Désirée practically plays in the mud as she plants and waters the vegetables in the garden. Marthe, recently a very devout Catholic, has virtually turned away from her large family in order to devote all possible time to the church and religious rites. She does not even tend to Désirée's need for a change of clothes. "Lorsqu'elle revenait de la messe, gardant dans ses cheveux les vagues parfums de l'église, elle était choquée de l'odeur puissante de terre que sa fille portait sur elle. ... elle ne pouvait la tolérer à côté d'elle, inquiétée par cette santé robuste." (216)

---

[1] Both the novelistic and essay passages on the suburbs have a literary forefather in Edmond et Jules de Goncourt, *Germinie Lacerteux* (Paris: Flammarion, 1921), p. 83.

Some natural phenomena elicit entirely different responses from the two protagonists of *Madeleine Férat*. This novelistic technique delineates clearly the feminine nervous system of Guillaume in contrast with the heroine's more masculine one. During a storm Madeleine is excited by the flashes of lightning, but the thunder and lightning frighten him (17-18). Her more aggressive male temperament also asserts itself when she seeks out the hot sun, while Guillaume is content to react passively to the cool, shady, and generally voluptuous aspects of nature. After walking for a while in the shade, Madeleine wants to step out into the sunshine again; "l'ombre finissait toujours par peser à cette nature puissante. Ils allaient au soleil, au grand soleil de juillet.... L'air brûlait. Madeleine marchait à l'aise dans cette fournaise ardente." (98) But the hot sun which revitalizes her, causes Guillaume to quickly gasp for breath, and they return to the cool shadows (98-99). After their marriage, the contrast between the two temperaments appears even greater: "Guillaume préférait l'hiver, l'air tiède et moite du foyer; mais Madeleine adorait toujours le soleil, le grand soleil qui lui mordait la nuque et qui donnait à son sang des battements tranquilles et forts." (111)

The hero of *Le Docteur Pascal*, who also thrives in the heat of nature, reacts differently to a majestic and massive canyon than do his passengers on a trip by landau to Les Tulettes. He alone is not awed into silence as they pass between the steep chasmal walls of the gorges of La Seille baking in the heavy torrid air of midafternoon. "Félicité ne desserra pas les lèvres.... Presque seul, Pascal causa, dans sa tendresse passionnée pour cette nature ardente, tendresse qu'il s'efforçait de faire partager à son neveu. Mais il avait beau s'exclamer, lui montrer ... la vie de ces roches elles-mêmes, de cette carcasse colossale et puissante de la terre, d'où l'on entendait monter un souffle: Maxime restait froid, pris d'une sourde angoisse, devant ces blocs d'une majesté sauvage, dont la masse l'anéantissait." (64)

A change in a character's mood can also alter his attitude toward nature. Failure and sorrow, in turn, affect adversely the customary affection of Lazare, of *La Joie de vivre*, for the sea. After he fails his university examinations and returns to his seaside home, he is bored by the presence of the sea and no longer considers the prospect of swimming in its cold waters. Years later when his mother lies dying, Lazare, in despair, begins again to walk beside the sea. Its immensity, a quality that pacified other Zola characters, overwhelms this protagonist now: "La mer immense l'irritait..., il s'était jeté dans les champs, il cherchait les coins perdus, afin de s'y sentir seul et caché." (192) And during those first days following his mother's death, Lazare tries to resume his long walks; but again the sea, unsympathetic to his sorrow, "l'irritait comme une force stupide. ... C'était trop grand, trop froid, et il se hâtait de rentrer, de s'enfermer, pour se sentir moins petit, moins écrasé entre l'infini de l'eau et l'infini du ciel." (206)

Boredom transforms a once exciting countryside into something irritating for the hero of *L'Œuvre*. After three years in the country near Bennecourt, Claude begins to long again for Paris. Consequently his and Christine's affection for their natural surroundings commences to deteriorate. They tire of the river; they no longer bother to row out to the little islands which formerly held so much charm for them. Now when walking along the river banks, "on y était grillé l'été, on s'y enrhumait l'hiver; et, quand au plateau, à ces vastes terres plantées de pommiers qui dominaient le village, elles devenaient comme un pays lointain, quelque chose de trop reculé, pour qu'on eût la folie d'y risquer ses jambes.... Ah! quelle usure mélancolique de l'habitude! comme l'éternelle nature avait l'air de se faire vieille, dans cette satiété lasse des mêmes horizons!" (181)

In two exceptional cases, characters who have developed a close affinity with nature temporarily lose perception of its phenomena. In one instance, Zola completely reverses his position that when a person falls in love, the physical senses respond sharply to stimuli from the outer world of nature. In "Les Quatre journées de Jean Gourdon", the youthful hero waits on the river bank to catch a glimpse of Babet. As she appears, his heart beats heavily, but "je ne sentais plus les fraîcheurs de la rosée" (CN II 429). Then, when he sees her running feet and her white stockings which the wind partially reveals, "je ne vis plus rien, ni la Durance, ni les saules, ni la blancheur du ciel. Je me moquais bien de la vallée! Elle n'était plus ma bonne amie; ses joies, ses tristesses me laissaient parfaitement froid. Que m'importaient mes camarades, les cailloux et les arbres des coteaux! La rivière pouvait s'en aller tout d'un trait si elle voulait; ce n'est pas moi qui l'aurais regrettée." (CN II 430) Actually the halt in the function of the physical senses is very brief, but Jean exploits the moment as a springboard to launch into sentimental expressions of his attraction to her. The action has quickly shifted from the sensorium to the heart. In effect, the young man simply replaces the object of his first love, nature, with a more mature love for woman. And, yet, at the same time, she incarnates nature: "Car Babet avait pris dans mon cœur la place de la vallée, Babet était le printemps." (CN II 430)

The second instance concerns Jean Macquart, of *La Terre*, who momentarily becomes impervious to nature. Zola points out in his notes for the novel that Jean, contrary to the other peasants, is to be sensitive to the countryside about him. Yet such is not the case when he learns of the murder of Hourdequin, his former employer: "Jean, qui s'était échappé de la cuisine, se retrouva en plaine rase, sous un ciel pluvieux de mars. Mais il ne voyait rien, bouleversé par cette histoire." (485) However, the numbing news easily justifies this particular exception.

The mood of two other characters in the same novel closely follows and imitates each change in the germinating grain. Buteau in particular enters into complete empathy with the grain he cultivates on his land. During a period of drought, he becomes unbearable as he suffers physically with the stunted, burned grains in his fields: "Il en souffrait positivement, comme les blés eux-mêmes, l'estomac rétréci, les membres noués de crampes, rapetissé, desséché de malaise et de colère." (204) But at a later date, he beams at the sight of the soil and reviving wheat which are avidly absorbing the rain that fell throughout the night. "Et lui, comme la terre, comme le blé, buvait par tous ses pores, détendu, rafraîchi, guéri." (205) Old Fouan appears at this moment. He, too, is "triste ou gai selon l'état des récoltes.... Cette pluie le ragaillardissait, lui aussi." (206)

Nature then is a mood setter. It can instigate a mood or intensify one. But a mood can also modify the typical reactions of a character to nature, although certain temperaments react atypically to natural phenomena.

Pascalian anguish besets man as he becomes aware of his insignificance, solitude, psychic discordancy and temporality in relation to the immense, harmonious, eternal universe. Often, in *La Terre*, Zola depicts the peasants as so many ants that labor on the gigantic earth. Elsewhere, the crushing immensity of the sky or sea appallingly reminds man of his disproportionate smallness. On the broad featureless plains or beneath the deep spacious sky, man discovers his own isolation even in the company of other human beings. Infinity reminds man of his finiteness, and his significance dwindles. He senses his solitude. Twilight and death of nature at autumn summon up melancholy in man. A wet, dismal winter depresses him. He is repelled by the nature that he himself has ravaged at the outskirts of a city, and his anxiety increases. The vast, heavy shroud of a cloud-laden sky threatens to enwrap man in its gray mass. As the dead ashes of dusk efface earth and sky, man apprehends the reality of death, and anguished hope arises for the return of light and life. A single star brings, perhaps, temporary consolation, as when the first evening star shines down on the two heroes of the "Aventures du grand Sidoine et du petit Médéric": "Et tous deux regardaient cette lueur consolatrice trouant d'un rayon d'espoir le voile morne du crépuscule." (CN 261) But the subsequent cosmic vitality of myriad stars in a nocturnal sky frightens Zola's humanity into the realization that man, however, is not ageless and that he is to enter into the black void of the earth. Morbidity and terror attend to his return to non-being.

V

PARTICIPANT IN LOVE

Les arbres se disaient tout bas de douces choses;
Les ruisseaux l'ont voulu, les fleurs l'ont comploté.
J'aime!

Hugo

The interrelationship of man and nature is often sensuous, sensual and, at times, erotic. To bridge such physical attraction, Zola often employs poetic anthropomorphism, that is to say, he attributes human characteristics, primarily human form, to something below humanity in the scale of being. Various phenomena of nature may then enjoy intimate relations among themselves or with human beings. Passionate abandon in nature takes place as early as in the short story "Simplice": "La mousse, ivre de rosée, s'y livrait à une débauche de croissance; les églantiers, allongeant leurs bras flexibles, se cherchaient dans les clairières pour exécuter des danses folles autour des grands arbres; les grands arbres eux-mêmes, tout en restant calmes et sereins, tordaient leur pied dans l'ombre et montaient en tumulte baiser les rayons d'été. ...la feuille embrassait le bois." (CN 65)

Most often nature displays its passion in order to set the stage for kindling and fanning the flames of love between man and woman. For example, in *La Faute de l'abbé Mouret*, roses anthropomorphize before the eyes of Serge and Albine who are about to fall in love. The girl has led the convalescing Serge into a veritable forest of roses where "certains coins d'ombre avaient des recueillements d'alcôve, une senteur d'amour, une tiédeur de bouquet pâmé aux seins d'une femme. Les rosiers avaient des voix chuchotantes" (170). Serge sleeps for a while there. Upon awakening within this thick rose bower, he becomes aware of Albine's physical beauty and tells her that he loves her. "Les fleurs vivantes s'ouvraient comme nudités, comme des corsages laissant voir les trésors des poitrines." (173) In fact, his new vision has transfigured all of the roses into sensual female flesh. More than a page is devoted to the description of different species of roses; selected examples follow: "...les roses thé prenaient des moiteurs adorables, étalaient des pudeurs cachées, des coins de corps qu'on ne montre pas, d'une finesse de soie, légèrement bleuis par le réseau des veines. ...le rose vif, fleurs en boutons de la gorge, fleurs à demi ouvertes des lèvres, soufflant le parfum d'une haleine tiède. ...des roses lie de vin, presque noires, saignantes, trouaient cette pureté d'épousée d'une blessure de passion. Noces du bois odorant, menant les virginités de mai aux fécondités de juillet et d'août; premier baiser ignorant, cueilli comme un bouquet, au matin du mariage." (173) At the same time, Albine seems to metamorphose into a large rose. "Et Serge le respirait, la mettait à sa poitrine." (174)

Nature usually anthropomorphizes first through lovers' senses of sight and touch. These senses operate frequently in combination and, therefore, will be incorporated in the first section, "Visions and Tactions". The subdivisions "Earth", "Sun", and "Water" isolate the chief natural phenomena that anthropomorphize for and, depending upon their gender in French, interract sensually with man or woman. In appearing to interrelate sensuously and even erotically with either, or both separately, nature sows the seed for instigating and advancing love between man and woman. Here the senses of hearing and smell, treated in separate sections entitled "Voices" and Scents", play dominant roles. Only the sense of taste plays a very minor role; since it generally unites in complicity with all the other senses, its function will be observed in the reviewing and concluding "General Remarks" of this chapter. The desired qualities that combine to make a natural setting ideal for lovers will unfold in the sections "Concealment" and "The Stream of Love".

But, first of all, let us consider the complicity which Zola assigns outright to nature in facilitating and furthering love for man and woman. Quite often he uses the word *accomplice* when nature activates the sensoria of lovers.

The hero of *La Confession de Claude*, tormented by his unrequited love for Laurence, recalls how self-sufficient a couple in love can be, whether in the midst of nature or among crowds of people: "Le ciel sourit, la terre se fait discrète, l'univers est complice." (119-120) In acknowledging the trees as "friends", it is evident that Guillaume of *Madeleine Férat* also recognizes the potential complicity of nature to hasten man's seduction of woman. Shortly after meeting Madeleine, Guillaume wishes to take her deep into the countryside, "non qu'il eût dessein de la faire tomber plus vite entre ses bras, mais parce qu'il aimait les arbres et qu'il désirait se promener avec elle à leur ombre" (65). In *La Fortune des Rougon* the author names the pleasant climate as "le grand coupable" that prompts lovers to frequent the semi-seclusion of the Saint-Mittre area and the out-skirts of Plassans on warm summer evenings (28).

The complicity of nature is stated more explicitly in *La Faute de l'abbé Mouret*. When Albine returns each evening to Serge from her frenzied, fruitless search for the legendary tree of the Paradou, "c'était tout le parc qui rentrait derrière elle, avec les souvenirs de leurs promenades, le lent éveil de leurs tendresses, au milieu de la nature complice" (245).

In his outline for the latter novel, Zola plots each evolving phase of Serge and Albine's love, from innocence through carnal possession, to take place in a certain propitious natural setting and at a specified hour of the day. He assigns to nature the role of advancing the couple's sensual-ity: "C'est par le paysage que les quatre amours changent." (432) Zola sketches the following:

9 heures. — Au verger. De purs enfants....
10 heures. — Les prairies. Des amoureux de douze ans, empressés, jouant à l'amourette.... *Le vague amour avant le sexe....*
12 heures. — La forêt. Le premier amour, l'adolescence encore discrète. Les rougeurs....
2 heures. — Les rochers. La flamme éclate (toujours ignorante). Soupirs tièdes. Nature plus ardente. Ils se perdent et se retrouvent avec un baiser brûlant qui leur donne un frisson. (423)

Many years later, the hero of *Le Docteur Pascal* will recall how Serge and Albine loved each other "au sein de la nature complice" (54).

1. VISIONS AND TACTIONS

> Les épaules d'argent de la Nuit qui frissonne
> Se couvrent de rougeur sous son premier baiser.
>
> Musset

a. *Earth*

> Et la terre est comme une épouse,
> Et l'homme est comme un fiancé!
>
> Hugo

The earth is consistently female throughout Zola's works. In the Preface to the *Contes à Ninon*, the author analyzes his "deep love" for the parched and severe Provençal countryside where he spent much of his youth. The first bond of affection bears resemblance to that shared by a child and his grandmother: "Sans doute, l'enfant rieur et les vieilles roches chagrines s'étaient autrefois pris de tendresse." (CN 52) In time the tenderness evolves into sensuous attraction to this countryside "qui flamboie au soleil, grise et nue, ... Je l'aime pour sa beauté âpre, ses roches désolées, ses thyms et ses lavandes." (CN 52) Thus his love for nature is conjured up by visual beauty, nudity, passionate warmth, and tantalizing scents, factors that frequently combine to arouse sexual desire in man.

Apparent anthropomorphosis of natural phenomena occurs when the author endows the Provençal landscape with the feminine contours and charms of his beloved Ninon. The girl of his dreams acquires at the same time certain aspects of the natural scene. Zola transfers the descriptive terms of the countryside to the human being and, consequently, sees in Ninon "la beauté désolée de ces collines, leur pâleur de marbre, rougissante aux derniers baisers du soleil" (CN 53). In exchange for the "passionate severities" that she appropriates from the countryside, the girl, on the other hand, endows nature with her grace. The voice of the stream, the glance of the stars, and the smiles of other natural phenomena are hers. The author tells Ninon that in looking at the valley, "je retrouvais tes lignes souples et fortes dans les ondulations des terrains" (CN 53). Even his love for the stones of the paths stems from "secret harmonies" that exist between Ninon and the landscape. Ninon and nature blend together as they interchange their attributes. This confusion of Ninon and a sensuous natural scene enhances the young man's infatuation for both.

When man imagines himself a giant, a sensual relationship with nature becomes more feasible. In the Preface to the *Nouveaux Contes à Ninon*, the author and Ninon feel possessive toward all nature, ranging from the sky down to the bare rocks. "Il me semblait, à cet âge, qu'en ouvrant les bras, j'allais prendre toute la campagne sur ma poitrine, pour lui donner un baiser de paix. Je me sentais des forces, des désirs, des bontés de géant." (CN 274) This image reappears in more grandiose proportions when Zola, with his mammoth need for creativity, expresses his literary frustration at not having accomplished anything he deems worthwhile in ten years of writing. Mere man is unable to attain the epic span sufficient to embrace and possess the entire earth: "...je me désole à penser que je n'ai pu étancher ma soif du vrai, que la grande nature échappe à mes bras trop courts. C'est l'âpre désir, prendre la terre, la posséder dans une étreinte, tout voir, tout dire." (CN 280)

A variation of this experience takes place in "Les Quatre journées de Jean Gourdon". As Jean proudly scans his lands, rich in fruit and grain,

he fancies his stature so gigantic that he could encompass all in his embrace (CN 453). Paternal pride in his vineyard and cultivated fields swells
within him as he feels the fecundity of the earth burst forth through the
soil and up into the blood of his own flesh. He enjoys the sensation of his
feet sinking into the soft earth (CN 453). This sensuous, almost sexual
pleasure of sensing one's feet sink into the earth explains that of the
heroine of *Madeleine Férat* when, in the course of her long cross-country
walk with Guillaume, she comes upon a mound of fine sandy soil into
which her feet sink. "Madeleine prit plaisir à choisir les places les plus
molles. Elle poussait de petits cris aigus en sentant ses bottines disparaî-
tre. Elle s'efforçait de faire de grandes enjambées, et elle riait de ne pou-
voir avancer, retenue par le terrain mouvant." (11) Here the author has
carefully chosen a noun of masculine gender, *le terrain*, in pointing up the
relationship with Madeleine, in contradistinction to *la terre* in the case of
Jean. In a later scene the earth becomes a gigantic, passionate woman
under the virile sun of summer: "...le ciel eut des caresses plus brûlantes,
...la terre devint femme, femme amoureuse et fécondée dont les entrailles
tressaillaient d'une puissante volupté dans le labeur de l'enfantement."
(98) Madeleine herself blossoms into mature womanhood at the same
time.

The blacksmith of the short story "Le Forgeron" derives vicarious
sensual pleasure from the "sacred task" performed by the plowshares
which he has personally forged. After each workday at the anvil, he sits in
front of his shop, overlooking the entire valley, and watches "la famille
nombreuse de ses charrues mordre le sol" (CN 360). From his high vantage point he feels possessive, in large measure, of all the farmers' cultivated plots of land lying below him. He loves the harvests, for they are like
daughters to him. The vicariousness of the smithy resembles that of the
tiller who digs into and impregnates the soil and who, when his labors
have fructified the earth, paternally admires his filial crops.

Object cathexis takes place in most of the preceding examples where the
libido is diverted to an object not directly sexual. However, in many of the
following passages, that object, some phenomenon of nature, will appear
to be sexual for man as he transfers his psychic energy into physical involvement for gratification.

The erotic relationship of man and earth is clearly defined in sexual
terms and imagery in *La Faute de l'abbé Mouret*. Frère Archangias tells
Abbé Mouret that any attempt to Christianize the Artauds is futile, for
they much prefer to labor in the rocky soil than attend Sunday mass. "Ils
forniqueraient avec leurs pièces de terre, tant ils les aiment!" (36) The

sounds of earth being spaded distract Abbé Mouret from the reading of his breviary on a lone walk in the arid countryside. "Les Artaud, en plein soleil, forniquaient avec la terre, selon le mot de Frère Archangias. C'étaient des fronts suants apparaissant derrière les buissons, des poitrines haletantes se redressant lentement, un effort ardent de fécondation." (41-42)

The friar's remark has primed unwittingly in the priest's imagination a new vision of the earth. As the remainder of the day draws on, the earth appropriates the carnality of a passionate woman. Each time a breath of hot air strikes his face, the priest looks up from his reading to seek the source of the "caress". But he does not perceive its origin "sur l'horizon enflammé, sur les lignes tordues de cette campagne de passion, séchée, pâmée au soleil, dans un vautrement de femme ardente et stérile" (41). Later, as the fiery sun sets upon the red earth, he and the friar watch the peasants return to their village. The cool night settles gradually, calming the earth. "Il y eut, par moments, un large soupir, comme si cette terre terrible, toute brûlée de passions, se fût enfin calmée, sous la pluie grise du crépuscule." (86-87)

The metamorphosis of the earth into female human form becomes more complete and detailed by moonlight than it was in sunlight or at twilight. A pale moon abets this anthropomorphosis for the priest who, some hours earlier, contracted a fever. Seeking temporary relief from his feverish condition, he opens a bedroom window onto the cool night but soon discerns in the moonlit landscape

... des blancheurs crayeuses pareilles à des vêtements de femme rejetés, découvrant des chairs noyées de ténèbres, assoupies dans les enfoncements des terrains. La nuit, cette campagne ardente prenait un étrange vautrement de passion. Elle dormait, débraillée, déhanchée, tordue, les membres écartés, tandis que de gros soupirs tièdes s'exhalaient d'elle, des aromes puissants de dormeuse en sueur. On eût dit quelque forte Cybèle tombée sur l'échine, la gorge en avant, le ventre sous la lune, soûle des ardeurs du soleil, et rêvant encore de fécondation. Au loin, le long de ce grand corps, l'abbé Mouret suivait des yeux le chemin des Olivettes, un mince ruban pâle qui s'allongeait comme le lacet flottant d'un corset. (128)

The priest is greatly alarmed by this seductive vision of an alluring and sensual sleeping goddess whose nudity the "silvery muslin" of the moon scarcely conceals. The earth transcends its female symbol and becomes woman anthropomorphically.

Later, the priest, now introduced as Serge, convalescing from his fever, experiences a strong desire to embrace nature. When he is first well enough to walk to the window and view the vast and beautiful Paradou, he opens his arms "comme pour serrer le jardin tout entier contre sa poitrine" (158). On his first venture outside the house, Albine props him against a mulberry tree facing the Paradou. Then, as nature arouses each of his five senses, he possesses more and more of the park. "Son corps entier entrait dans la possession de ce bout de nature, l'embrassait de ses membres; ses lèvres le buvaient, ses narines le respiraient; il l'emportait dans ses oreilles, il la cachait au fond de ses yeux. C'était à lui." (165) This masculine desire to embrace and possess the earth is experienced to a certain degree by Albine, too, shortly before she commits suicide by suffocation from the overpowering scents of flowers and other plants. After carrying all the flowers from the flowerbed into her room, "elle s'attaqua aux herbes, aux verdures; elle rampa, la poitrine contre le sol, cherchant dans une suprême étreinte de passion à emporter la terre elle-même" (389).

The erotic feelings of the peasant for his plot of earth assert themselves often throughout *La Terre*. In his intimate, lifelong contact with the soil, the peasant remains stubbornly amorous of the earth. For him the meanings of 'to own' and 'to ravish' fuse in the verb *possesser*. This possessive attitude toward the earth and his general insensitivity to its intrinsic beauty no doubt explain why the earth does not anthropomorphize for the peasant, even when the latter considers and covets it as his 'mistress' or 'wife'.

Passion for the earth is very real for the seventy-year old Fouan who has expended and exhausted his physical energies "dans une passion de la terre si âpre, que son corps se courbait, comme pour retourner à cette terre, violemment désirée et possédée" (24). Because of old age, Fouan, like his father before him, decides to divide his land among his progeny. Together with his two sons and one daughter, he calls on Baillehache to draw up the necessary legal document. Inwardly, Fouan feels "le déchirement de tout son corps, à se séparer de ces biens si chaudement convoités avant la mort de son père, cultivés plus tard avec un acharnement de rut…. Il avait aimé la terre en femme qui tue et pour qui on assassine…. Et voilà qu'il avait vieilli, qu'il devait céder cette maîtresse à ses fils, comme son père la lui avait cédée à lui-même, enragé de son impuissance." (26)

One wintry evening when his family and some neighbors gather together in the warmth of the stable, Fouan explains that the passionate love of the peasants for the earth began in feudal times: "…la terre, fécondée de son effort, passionnément aimée et désirée pendant cette intimité chaude de chaque heure, comme la femme d'un autre que l'on soigne, que l'on ne peut posséder." (82-83) Yet the earth has always remained indifferent and never rewarded even a single surplus grain to the peasant during the latter's one-sided lifelong love affair. "...il s'était donné tout entier à la terre, qui, après l'avoir à peine nourri, le laissait misérable, inassouvi, honteux d'impuissance sénile, et passait aux bras d'un autre mâle, sans pitié même pour ses pauvres os, qu'elle attendait." (83)

Even the more educated landowner, Hourdequin, is enamoured of the earth in much the same way as the peasant. As a young boy, the earth offered him freedom and often lured him from school. But as a young man, "il l'avait aimée en amoureux, son amour s'était mûri, comme s'il l'eût prise dès lors en légitime mariage, pour la féconder. Et cette tendresse ne faisait que grandir, à mesure qu'il lui donnait son temps, son argent, sa vie entière, ainsi qu'à une femme bonne et fertile, dont il excusait les caprices, même les trahisons. Il s'emportait bien des fois, lorsqu'elle se montrait mauvaise, lorsque, trop sèche ou trop humide, elle mangeait les semences, sans rendre des moissons; puis, il doutait, il en arrivait à s'accuser de mâle impuissant ou maladroit: la faute en devait être à lui, s'il ne lui avait pas fait un enfant." (104)

Sexual involvement with the earth also creates strong desire in Buteau. This eroticism is especially evident when he comes into ownership of a plot of land. The earth being his alone to plow, "il voulait la pénétrer, la féconder jusqu'au ventre" (200). Like a lover, he visits his fields of wheat and oats even when they require no tending, simply to look at them. Following the murder of Françoise, the Buteaus repossess the widower Jean's house and land, by claiming that the property reverts to the family. Buteau passionately rejoices at the prospect of possessing more earth. "Toute sa chair s'était mise à trembler de joie, comme au retour d'une femme désirée et qu'on a crue perdue." (480)

For old Fouan, the earth becomes an ungrateful and deceiving mistress. Fallen ill, he resents furiously the document he drew up with old Saucisse, though ten years his junior, whereby the latter has willed an acre of land upon his death to the former, provided Fouan pay fifteen sous each day that Saucisse lives. Fouan now regards this document as "une vraie bêtise de vieux passionné donnant ses derniers sous pour retourner en secret à la gueuse qui le trompe.... Ça devait le tenir bien fort, ce furieux désir de posséder, qu'ils ont dans les os comme une rage, tous les anciens mâles, usés à engrosser la terre." (340) In spite of his advanced age and waning strength, the decrepit Fouan persists in tottering out for his daily visits with the plots of earth he once owned, "dans cette manie des vieux passionnés que hantent leurs maîtresses d'autrefois" (431). He is saddened that this thankless and fickle mistress, to whom he had given his strength, love, and life, has already forgotten him and has now slipped into the arms of another male.

Whereas Fouan simply expects to rot away in this 'indifferent' earth after his death, the earth appears compassionate when it tenderly receives the body of another seventy-year old peasant, in the fifth section of "Comment on meurt". Jean-Louis Lacour is buried in the earth which he knew so well and loved, and which shared his sentiments: "Leurs tendresses devaient finir par là, la terre devait le prendre et le garder." (CN II 608)

Man's sexual relationship with the earth seems literally to reach orgasmic fulfillment in the scene from *La Terre* where Jean makes love to Françoise during the wheat harvest. Afraid to be left with child, she asks him to withdraw. Thus, in onanism, man sows the earth with his own seed, thereby bringing to an apogee the erotic relationship between man and the female earth and his constant efforts to fecundate her, because "la terre, ...elle ne se refuse jamais, le flanc ouvert à tous les germes, éternellement féconde" (248).

b. Sun

Soleil, premier amour de toute créature!

Lamartine

Zola attributes male aggressiveness and ardor to the sun. For a long time the sun was the only master of the Paradou in *La Faute de l'abbé Mouret*. Each morning the vast garden watched the sun "sauter le mur de clôture de ses rayons obliques, s'asseoir d'aplomb à midi sur la terre pâmée, s'en aller le soir, à l'autre bout, en un baiser d'adieu rasant les feuillages" (236). Sensuous and erotic imagery characterizes the descriptions of the sunsets that impress Albine and Serge on their first walks in the park (234).

The sun can be passionate toward both the female earth and a receptive human being. With its ardent caresses, the sun fructifies the former and implants health and vigor in the latter. The hero of *La Confession de Claude* remembers how the Provençal countryside, "âpre et douce pour ceux qui se sont pénétrés de ses ardeurs et de ses tendresses", lies prostrate under the hot midday sun, "heure virile et forte, donnant au sang une maturité précoce et à la terre des entrailles fécondes" (64).

However, most often the virile sun appears to caress only the human being, particularly woman, with its rays. The heroine of *Madeleine Férat*, who has a predilection for walking under the hot July sun, yields metaphorically to those caresses: "...elle laissait voluptueusement le soleil mordre son cou et ses bras nus; ...elle s'abandonnait aux caresses de l'astre." (98) She is like the dormant, winter-stricken bush whose energy and vigor are revitalized by the summer sun (97).

The phenomenon of a virile sun implanting its life-giving force into woman, likened to a plant again, occurs repeatedly in *Le Docteur Pascal*. One afternoon Pascal and Clotilde walk along the dry, dusty road to La Séguiranne. The couple thrive in the bare, burning arid landscape with its occasional, stunted almond and olive trees. Exposed to the sunlit "flame of a perpetual passion", Clotilde and Pascal become "more alive and beautiful" as they sense the hot rays seep into their veins. "Elle, abritée un peu par son ombrelle, s'épanouissait, heureuse de ce bain de lumière, ainsi qu'une plante de plein midi; tandis que lui, refleurissait, sentait la sève brûlante du sol lui remonter dans les membres, en un flot de virile joie." (189) Even though the simile includes Pascal, a man, the stress is shifted in his case from the sun to the feminine noun 'sap', which he feels rising from the soil. Upon arrival at La Séguiranne they see Sophie kissing her fiancé. And in a variation on the above theme, the healthy Sophie seems to have received direct nutriment from the sun and also the soil out of which she appears to have grown: "Certainement, Sophie avait encore grandi en santé et en beauté, sauvée du mal héréditaire, poussée solidement comme un de ces arbres, les pieds dans l'herbe humide des sources, la tête nue au grand soleil." (190) In an earlier scene, Maxime, whom Clotilde has not seen in years, remarks how well she looks. She attributes her good health to life in the sunshine; Dr. Pascal corroborates her observation by adding that, like the trees, one's health is dependent upon the sun (62).

The solar virility is tempered for the sick, whom the sun regenerates. One day in August while the sickly Jeanne, of *Une Page d'amour*, is seated on the grass in the Deberles' garden she takes pleasure in watching the warm sunshine slowly creep up her legs, caressing her body (190). In "Le Printemps — journal d'un convalescent", Zola writes that on his first day of convalesence the rays of the sun spread themselves over the bed, warming his hands, and "kissing" his fingers. "Et, pendant longtemps, je me suis laissé pénétrer par les tièdes clartés, m'abandonnant au printemps, puisant dans son premier appel la force d'aller à lui." (LFAM 427) Thus, aided by the sun, the convalescent yields to spring; but a second union is consummated with the sun itself as it approaches the horizon: "Ses rayons tièdes me touchaient en plein visage et m'unissaient à lui." (LFAM 428)

The convalescing hero of *La Faute de l'abbé Mouret* is also caressed by the warm sunshine; but in this later work, feminine nouns, replacing the earlier masculine ones, are used for the natural phenomena that interrelate erotically with man. During the morning hours, Serge watches the rays of the sun advance very slowly toward him. "C'était ... une approche d'amoureuse, étirant ses membres blonds, s'allongeant jusqu'à l'alcôve d'un mouvement rythmé, avec une lenteur voluptueuse qui donnait un désir fou de sa possession. Enfin, vers deux heures, la nappe de soleil quitta le dernier fauteuil, monta le long des couvertures, s'étala sur le lit, ainsi qu'une chevelure dénouée. Serge abandonna ses mains amaigries de convalescent à cette caresse ardente, il fermait les yeux à demi, il sentait courir sur chacun de ses doigts des baisers de feu, il était dans un bain de lumière, dans une étreinte d'astre." (152-153) Thus, the virile sun of the outdoors has changed sex upon entering the hero's bedroom to become *la nappe de soleil*, a tempting *amoureuse* for Serge. There may be a technical lapsus in a following sentence where Serge watches the slow departure of *le soleil* from the bed and across the furniture "avec le regret de ne l'avoir pas retenu sur sa poitrine" (153). But the relationship between a natural phenomenon of one gender and a human being of the opposite sex is resumed as Serge subsequently projects and loses himself in the gradually paling sky which, masculine in gender, is now softly tinted in rose, lavender, and yellow, becoming "une chair vivante, une vaste nudité immaculée qu'un souffle faisait battre comme une poitrine de femme" (153).

c. *Water*

> Où la terre embrasse dans l'ombre
> Les replis sinueux des eaux.
>
> Lamartine

Bodies of water, unlike the female earth and the male sun, change sex symbols, depending upon the sex and maturity of the human being with whom they come in contact.[1] Zola evokes female nudity in describing certain currents. Slow flowing streams and rivers, as well as quick tum-

---

[1] Traditionally in literature writers tend to designate the female symbol consciously or unconsciously to water. See Gaston Bachelard, *L'Eau et les Rêves, Essai sur l'imagination de la matière* (Paris: Corti, 1942).

bling waters from natural springs, can suggest the limbs of nude women. An example of each kind is found in *La Faute de l'abbé Mouret*. Serge and Albine follow a lazily flowing river downstream; "ils voyaient l'eau nue, sur le lit des herbes, étirer ses membres purs, s'endormir en plein soleil du sommeil souple" (208). Another time they come upon a number of refreshing springs. "...elles allongeaient des bras d'une blancheur pure; elles rebondissaient, pareilles à des nudités joueuses d'enfant; elles tombaient brusquement en une chute, dont la courbe molle semblait renverser un torse de femme d'une chair blonde." (227)

Zola feels a sensual attraction toward the river, much as he would toward a woman. A formative stage of this feeling may have appeared around the age of sixteen when Zola would meet his friends beside a river, "car nous étions pris alors de la passion de l'eau" (DL 74). He also recalls how, after he returned to Paris from boating with friends on the Seine, he would generally look down at the river with a look of a "jealous lover" (CN I 77). In "Souvenirs", he writes: "Quand je passe sur les ponts, par ces soirées ardentes, la Seine m'appelle avec des grondements d'amitié. Elle coule, large, fraîche, pleine de lenteurs amoureuses, s'offrant, s'attardant entre les quais. L'eau a des froissements de jupes moirées. C'est une amante souple, dans laquelle on a des désirs irrésistibles de 'piquer une tête'." (CN 386)

The author derives much pleasure from his predawn visits to an enclosed public swimming pool in the Seine. Then the pool is practically deserted. "L'eau est plus fraîche, après le sommeil de la nuit. Elle est plus pure, plus vierge." (CN 387) At that early hour he enjoys especially the stroll along the quais, "en regardant l'eau, de ce regard de convoitise des amants. Elle va être à vous. Dans le bain, l'eau dort. C'est vous qui la réveillez. Vous pouvez la prendre entre vos bras, en silence. Vous sentez le courant s'en aller tout du long de votre chair, de la nuque aux talons, avec une caresse fuyante." (CN 387) As the sun rises, "un frisson court sur la peau avec les baisers plus vifs de la rivière" (CN 397). But as soon as the bathers begin to arrive in throngs, Zola departs. "La rivière n'est plus la vierge du petit jour; elle est la fille de midi qui se donne à tous, qui est meurtrie, toute chaude des embrassements de la foule." (CN 388)

It is also at a very early hour that the hero of "Les Quatre journées de Jean Gourdon", seemingly beckoned by the murmurs of the Durance, arises from bed to go down to the river one spring morning (427). The gentle, cheerful, white countenance of the river particularly impresses the youth (429). Time alters their relationship; and Jean avows many years later that "la Durance, ma première amante, était maintenant pour moi

une bonne mère qui semblait se plaire à rendre mes champs gras et fertiles"
(CN 448).

The "amitiés sauvages" which the heroine of *Thérèse Raquin* felt as a
young girl toward the Seine are revived years later on the all-day outings
at Saint-Ouen with her husband Camille. She keeps her hands in the
current and allows her dress to be torn and soiled by the stones and thick
mud of the river banks (62). The imagery seems to couch a repressed wish
on the part of Thérèse to be ravished by the river itself. The affectionate
ties between the Seine and Renée and her sister as young girls are less
'wild' in *La Curée*. Toward the end of the novel Renée goes up to their
former playroom on the top floor of the Hôtel Béraud, situated on the Ile
Saint-Louis. She is calmed by the view of the Seine flowing toward her,
"comme en ces heureux temps où elle avait peur de la voir grossir et monter jusqu'à la fenêtre. Elle se souvenait de leurs tendresses pour la rivière,
de leur amour de sa coulée colossale, de ce frisson de l'eau grondante,
s'étalant en nappe à leurs pieds, s'ouvrant autour d'elles, derrière elles, en
deux bras qu'elles ne voyaient plus, et dont elles sentaient encore la grande
et pure caresse." (308-309)

The sea, too, is a majestic, affectionate friend for Pauline Quenu, in
La Joie de vivre. She enjoys swimming in the open sea, and when tired,
floats on her back. The sex symbols of the sea and its waters fluctuate for
Pauline, a young girl at the time. "Cette mer qui la berçait, était restée sa
grande amie. Elle en aimait l'haleine âpre, le flot glacé et chaste, elle
s'abandonnait à elle, heureuse d'en sentir le ruissellement immense contre
sa chair, goûtant la joie de cet exercice violent, qui réglait les battements
de son cœur." (76) Unlike this large comrade, the sea will loom as a
gigantic lover for the more mature heroine of "Les Coquillages de M.
Chabre", in the next section on "Sounds".

Similarly, the river becomes masculine for Miette, in *La Fortune des
Rougon*. The shift to a male symbol befits the heroine's recent physical
maturation. After Silvère teaches Miette to swim, she responds voluptuously to the sensual, almost sexual carressing of the waters of the stream.
While the feminine words *la rivière* and *l'eau* designate almost exclusively
the flowing waters in the foregoing examples, the masculine words *le flot*
and *le courant* now become the dominant appellations of the stream as it
interacts physically with Miette:

Libre de ses membres, bercée par le flot, jouant avec lui, elle se laissait envahir
par les souplesses molles de la rivière, par le silence du ciel, par les rêveries des
berges mélancoliques.... La rivière surtout, cette eau, ce terrain mouvant, la
portait avec des caresses infinies. Elle éprouvait, quand elle remontait le courant,

une grande jouissance à sentir le flot filer plus rapide contre sa poitrine et contre ses jambes; c'était un long chatouillement, très doux, qu'elle pouvait supporter sans rire nerveux. Elle s'enfonçait davantage, se mettait de l'eau jusqu'aux lèvres, pour que le courant passât sur ses épaules, l'enveloppât d'un trait, du menton aux pieds, de son baiser fuyant. Elle avait des langueurs qui la laissaient immobile à la surface, tandis que de petits flots glissaient mollement entre son costume et sa peau, gonflant l'étoffe; puis elle se roulait dans les nappes mortes, ainsi qu'une chatte sur un tapis. (221-222)

This same river will be examined as an accomplice of love in a following section, "The Stream of Love". In its role of active complicity, nature will continue to play upon the visual and tactile senses; but it will concentrate even more on the auditory and olfactory.

2. VOICES

> Ce que le flot dit aux rivages,
> Ce que le vent dit aux vieux monts,
> Ce que l'astre dit aux nuages,
> C'est le mot ineffable: Aimons!
>
> Hugo

Chateaubriand demonstrated the evocative power of sounds in nature, sounds that reverberate in turn in the texture of his descriptions, to arouse sensory images. Natural phenomena in all forms speak clearly and frequently in many works of the French romantic poets. For Zola, nature attains varying degrees of articulation as it appears to communicate with man. Zola often exploits the very suggestive quality of the auditory sense of lovers when he attributes voices to nature.

It is primarily through its sounds that the sea becomes an accomplice of love, as in *Les Mystères de Marseille*. One Sunday afternoon Marius arrives earlier than usual to wait for Fine by the sea at Saint-Henri. He sits down on a cliff and is soon lost in tender thoughts of love. "L'immense horizon l'attendrissait; ...la mer et le ciel, l'infini des eaux et de l'air le troublaient, lui ouvraient l'âme." (201) Fine arrives and sits beside him. A serene twilight spreads around them. "Il y avait des souffles de tendresse dans l'air, une grande voix frissonnante qui allait en s'éteignant." (201) Marius tells her that just before her arrival, the waves confided a secret to him. "Je ne sais ce qu'ont la mer et le ciel ce soir. Ils parlent d'une voix si douce qu'ils ont ému mon cœur et troublé mon esprit." (203) The sounding waves of the sea, repeating her name, had revealed his love for Fine.

"L'heure était douce pour un aveu d'amour. Une tendresse divine, un calme souriant sortait de la grande mer attendrie. Au pied de la falaise, les vauges battaient lentement, berçant la côte qui sommeillait; tandis que, de la terre, chaude encore et fiévreuse, venaient des souffles âpres de passion. On eût dit que la grande mer appuyait de sa voix les tendres paroles de Marius." (203) The "monotonous voice" of the sea seems to "lull" the avowals of love that the couple exchange (205). Even after their marriage, Marius and Fine spend evenings beside the sea in a gesture of gratitude to its earlier complicity and also to seek "dans ses voix profondes le chant qui convenait à leurs amours. Quand ils s'en retournaient, ils s'aimaient davantage, ils goûtaient des nuits plus heureuses." (322)

The steady rhythmic beating sounds of the sea almost precipitate an adulterous love affair in *La Joie de vivre*. Lazare has returned to his seaside home where his wife Louise is expecting their child. He and Pauline renew their childhood escapades along the coast. The intoxicating salty air calls to mind tender memories from earlier years, and "la mer semblait les bercer et les alanguir de l'éternelle monotonie de sa voix" (285). Then one evening at home, Lazare nearly succeeds in seducing Pauline when "cette grande paix frissonnante de la nuit, où montait seulement la plainte accoutumée de la marée haute, les avait peu à peu pénétrés d'une sorte d'attendrissement sensuel" (291).

By means of its sounds the sea seems almost to become a gigantic lover for the heroine of the short story "Les Coquillages de M. Chabre". While at the seaside resort of Piriac, Estelle Chabre meets Hector, a young man who swims with her each day and who brings various shellfish for her middle-aged husband. Chabre's doctor has recommended the consumption of shellfish to induce fertility. Ideal weather and swimming conditions abet Estelle and Hector's flirtation. One evening as the three sit on the beach, Hector at Estelle's feet, the sound and movement of the incoming tide cause Estelle's mind to slip suggestively into daydreams of passion. "La mer montait, avec un large bruit de caresse. On aurait dit une voix de passion, quand la vague battait le sable; puis, cette voix s'apaisait tout d'un coup, et le cri se mourait avec l'eau qui se retirait, dans un murmure plaintif d'amour dompté. La jeune femme rêvait d'être aimée ainsi, par un géant dont elle aurait fait un petit garçon." (CN I 234)

Voices from the nature within the Clos-Marie, a vast natural garden, seem to announce to Angélique of *Le Rêve* that the arrival of her Prince Charming, whom she has been awaiting for years, is imminent. Immersed in the strange saintly world of Jacques de Voragine's *La Légende dorée*, Angélique is convinced that the leaves, the stream, and even the stones of the cathedral are speaking to her. The human ear attunes slowly to the articulation of natural phenomena, so Angélique has initial difficulty in deciphering such utterances. Her dream materializes slowly in the Clos-Marie setting. She falls in love with Félicien, and hears the surrounding trees and stones sanction their love (152). However, Félicien's father arranges for him to marry Claire de Voincourt, and then Angélique regards the Clos-Marie as "un coin de nature ami refusant d'être complice" (161). No more whispering voices reach her ears (165). Angélique falls deathly ill. Félicien climbs up into her room one night and almost persuades her to flee far away with him. But at the last moment Angélique decides against the flight and bids him to listen to the Clos-Marie which counsels her not to go against his father's wish. The plants and trees, the 'singing' stream, the air and even the stones of the cathedral join voices to caution her and to affirm that love will triumph ultimately (180).

A forest, however, advises against love in the short story "Simplice". The hero abandons the royal court to live in the forest. He, too, has initial difficulty in understanding the voices of nature. The first new language he learns is the insects' concise idiom where a single sound, through variations in pitch and length, designates many things. Then he abandons the language of man. And as soon as he can communicate with the trees and flowers, he chats incessantly with the forest.[2] The prince meets and falls in love with the undine Fleur-des-Eaux; but the forest is deeply perturbed, for it knows that a kiss exchanged with a mortal being would be fatal not only for him but also for the ethereal undine, whom the forest considers as its very soul. When Simplice does not desist in his persistent pursuit to reach her, the brambles wrap their thorny arms about him, the branches of bushes stiffen and entwine themselves into tighter and more resistant masses, the moss makes itself slippery, and rocks roll into his path. And the forest vocally pleads in vain (CN 69-70).

The voices of nature in *La Faute de l'abbé Mouret* also do not enunciate their message clearly in the beginning phases of Serge and Albine's love. Only as the climactic moment of sexual union approaches will the lovers unmistakably comprehend the Paradou's intent for them. Initial awareness of the efforts of the park to communicate with them follows the couple's first kiss. "Maintenant, elle [la vie du parc] les assourdissait par instants, elle leur parlait une langue qu'ils n'entendaient pas, elle leur adressait des sollicitations, auxquelles ils ne savaient comment céder."

[2] Nature converses articulately with man in the short story "Le Sous-préfet aux champs", the second part of "Ballades en prose", by a fellow 'naturalist', Alphonse Daudet, *Lettres de mon moulin* (Paris: Charpentier, 1922), pp. 165-171.

(236) Troubled by the voices and scents of the Paradou, the pair barricade themselves in Serge's room and try to suppress the existence of the park by not talking about it. But the presence and strong vitality of nature penetrate the closed windows and drawn curtains. While scents seep in through cracks, "des voix prolongées faisaient sonner les vitres; toute la vie du dehors riait, chuchotait, embusquée sous les fenêtres" (239).

Albine finally discovers the legendary tree of the Paradou and convinces Serge to follow her there. As they walk through the garden, the latter voices its approval in what sounds like "un rire prolongé, un murmure satisfait volant de feuille en feuille, jusqu'au bout des avenues les plus profondes" (249). Nature guides them; branches indicate the way while bushes raise a barrier behind them to prevent their turning back. The gigantic and fantastic tree exudes a heavy, heady voluptuousness that intimates an "ardent mating" of nature, now "sated in the arms of the sun". Through its distended bark oozes a seductive sap that diffuses over the surrounding area: "Par moments, les reins de l'arbre craquaient; ses membres se roidissaient comme ceux d'une femme en couches; la sueur de vie, qui coulait de son écorce, pleuvait plus largement sur les gazons d'alentour, exhalant la mollesse d'un désir, noyant l'air d'abandon, pâlissant la clairière d'une jouissance." (251) Some of its effusing essence transfuses to Serge, who kisses Albine passionately and tells her how much he adores her. The sounds of nature become more audible as the moment of seduction approaches. Albine joyfully indulges in the sensation of having Serge at her mercy and of hearing "le jardin se réjouir de son triomphe, l'aider d'une clameur lentement grossie" (253).

In no uncertain terms "la faute de l'abbé Mouret" is willed, fostered, and precipitated by nature itself. This is explicit as Albine, now breathless, beckons Serge to listen to the voices of nature: "C'était le jardin qui avait voulu la faute. Pendant des semaines, il s'était prêté au lent apprentissage de leur tendresse.... Maintenant, il était le tentateur, dont toutes les voix enseignaient l'amour." (254) Voluptuous fragrances arrive from the flower garden and the orchard, and from the prairies come sighs of grasses. "La forêt soufflait la passion géante des chênes, les chants d'orgue des hautes futaies, une musique solennelle, menant le mariage des frênes, des bouleaux, des charmes, des platanes, au fond des sanctuaires de feuillage.... Et, dans cet accouplement du parc entier, les étreintes les plus rudes s'entendaient au loin, sur les roches, là où la chaleur faisait éclater les pierres gonflées de passion, où les plantes épineuses aimaient d'une façon tragique, sans que les sources voisines pussent les soulager, tout allumées elles-mêmes par l'astre qui descendait dans leur lit." (254) The animals and even the very atoms of matter itself support the universal summons to make love. "Ce fut l'arbre qui confia à l'oreille d'Albine ce que les mères murmurent aux épousées, le soir des noces." (255) As Albine gives herself to Serge, all in nature lend their concerted cry of passion and victory. "Le parc applaudissait formidablement." (255)

3. SCENTS

Les tièdes voluptés des nuits mélancoliques
Sortaient autour de nous du calice des fleurs.

Musset

The much demonstrated complicity of nature seems to work best in the immediacy of the olfactory sense for the lovers in Zola's works. Scents in nature soften the heart, advance the progress of love, and often precipitate the sexual act.

The odor of spring greenery brings tears to those tenderly inclined toward love. In *La Conquête de Plassans*, the forty-year old Mme Mouret, enamored of her priest, weeps like a young girl when the smell of freshly trimmed hedges reaches her nostrils (154). As Angélique of *Le Rêve* reaches the age of sixteen and feels herself blossoming into womanhood, the odors from sprouting greenery bring tears to her eyes, while lilac and laburnum scents make the blood rush to her cheeks (57-58). In the short story "Madame Neigeon", Georges de Vaugelade maneuvers a second meeting with the heroine at the races. The two walk slowly together, her arm linked in his. Nearby the apple trees are in bloom. "Et, surtout, ce qui m'attendrissait aux larmes, c'était l'odeur de primtemps répandue autour de nous, montant des herbes, aux deux bords de la route." (CN I 199).

The pervading odor of greenery advances the love idyll of the heroine of *Nana* with the young Georges Hugon at her country estate. She becomes like a young girl in the open air; "et le soir, grise de l'odeur des feuilles, elle montait rejoindre son Zizi, caché derrière le rideau, ça lui semblait une escapade de pensionnaire en vancances" (172).

Plant scents play an extremely significant role in *La Faute de l'abbé Mouret*. A bouquet of roses moves the bedridden Serge to tears. (155) Once well enough to go outside, he wants to walk to a certain thicket of roses; but Albine counsels him to wait. "Le parfum des roses est trop fort pour toi. Je n'ai jamais pu m'asseoir sous les rosiers, sans me sentir toute lasse, la tête perdue, avec une envie très douce de pleurer." (168) Another day she does lead him through the vast beds of flowers in the Paradou.

They come upon an old colonnade in ruins and sit down on one of the fallen pillars. Clumps of lilies surround them. "Les lis leur offraient un refuge de candeur, après leur promenade d'amants, au milieu de la sollicitation ardente des chèvrefeuilles suaves, des violettes masquées, des verveines exhalant l'odeur fraîche d'un baiser, des tubéreuses soufflant la pâmoison d'une volupté mortelle. Les lis, aux tiges élancées, les mettaient dans un pavillon blanc, sous le toit de neige de leurs calices, seulement égayés des gouttes d'or légères des pistils. Et ils restaient, ainsi que des fiancés d'enfants, souverainement pudiques, comme au centre d'une tour de pureté, d'une tour d'ivoire inattaquable." (187) Albine, whose name means 'white', and whom Zola, in his notes, had first called "Blanche", like the heroine of *Les Mystères de Marseille*, becomes as white as the lilies themselves. Imbued until evening with the crystal purity of the lilies, the couple depart with the innocence of ten-year old children (188). This action is to some degree a variant on that theme of purification where the human being assimilates purity from nature.

On another morning as Albine and Serge walk in the Paradou, the hot sun forces the languidly strolling couple to seek the shady areas. The deeper they penetrate the cool forest, the more their pace slackens. The odors from the trees cause tears to well up in the eyes of both (216). Moreover, these odors contribute to the lovers' sensation of imminent entry into some "redoubtable happiness" (217).

The perfume of flowers advances the love of Hélène Grandjean and Henri Deberle in *Une Page d'amour*. Love begins to take shape in the heroine's mind one morning in early spring. Reclining on a chaise longue, Hélène alternately reads from *Ivanhoe* and watches the shifting rising mists cloak and disclose various sections of an ethereal Paris. She ponders over the possibility in actual life of an all-consuming love, such as is found in Walter Scott's novel. The word *aimer* tenderly taunts Hélène as the rays of the sun melt down the lake of fog to gradually reveal the real city. Her daughter Jeanne brings in a big bunch of yellow stock whose scent perfumes the entire room. Hélène presses Jeanne tightly to her bosom as if to convince herself that her great love is for her daughter, whereas it is in fact for Henri. "Cette matinée de printemps, cette grande ville si douce, ces premières giroflées qui lui parfumaient les genoux, avaient peu à peu fondu son cœur." (71)

Throughout the month of May, Hélène, her daughter, and Mme Deberle attend the special evening services dedicated to the Virgin Mary. Reinforced by the religious chants, the heavy and heady scents of the profuse bouquets of roses placed around the statue of the Virgin Mary sharpen Hélène's senses, but dull her mind, troubled during the day by thoughts about Henri. Usually the doctor is waiting outside the church to escort the trio, and he is there even on that evening when his wife does not attend the ceremonies in order to accompany Hélène and her daughter to their home. The three wind their way along the silent and deserted Rue Raynouard. Their pace slackens as the fragrances of lilacs and other flowers in bloom lade the warm, mild spring air. When they hear old Mme Fétu saying her rosary behind them, Jeanne runs back to give her a coin, leaving Hélène and Henri alone for a few moments. "Par terre, les marronniers avaient laissé tomber une pluie de leurs petites fleurs, et ils marchaient sur ce tapis rose. Puis ils s'arrêtèrent, le cœur trop gonflé pour aller plus loin." (154)

The sight of cut roses in Les Halles recalls to Zola's mind a certain walk with Ninon along a path bordered by fields of violets, whose penetrating, sweet scents overpower the girl. "Tu t'appuyais sur mon bras toute pâmée, comme endormie d'amour par l'odeur douce." (CN 404)

Flower scents render the heroine of *Madeleine Férat* vulnerable for seduction by her former lover. During the morning hours, preceding her visit with Jacques, she strolls beneath a warm spring sun in the flower market at the Madeleine, where the fragrances of the flowers amass to sensually caress her body:

Un parfum pénétrant flottait à ses pieds, s'élevait le long de ses jupes avec des ivresses molles; il lui semblait que ce parfum arrivé à la hauteur de ses lèvres brûlait sa face doucement comme une caresse. Peu à peu, ses joues étaient devenues roses, ses lèvres avaient eu un vague sourire. Le printemps battait dans ses veines, montait à sa tête. Elle était toute étourdie, comme si elle se fût penchée sur une cuve.
... Ivre du parfum des fleurs, attiédie par le soleil, elle continua à marcher, s'abandonna à une rêverie douce et fuyante. (275-276)

Gradually the image of Guillaume and their life together fades into one of Jacques and other April mornings shared in the Verrières woods. Suddenly aware that passersby are glancing curiously at her, she directs her steps elsewhere, but returns unintentionally to the flower market. "Elle s'y oubliait de nouveau, au milieu des souffles tièdes et parfumés, retrouvant ses sensations d'évanouissements voluptueux." (276) Noticing that it is almost noon, she rushes to the apartment of Jacques, who is surprised to see her and asks a number of questions. But, being short of breath and still feeling somewhat giddy, she cannot reply. A wilting bouquet of flowers on the mantelpiece redirects her thoughts to the flower market, and she smiles. The smile is still on her lips as she turns toward Jacques, intending to tell him of her marriage to Guillaume; but his arm already encircles her waist, and she yields unhesitatingly.

Even odors of marine plant life can be an accomplice of love. In "Naïs Micoulin", the heroine and Frédéric Rostand often sit beside the sea during their month-long courtship. "Une odeur pénétrante d'herbes marines les grisait de désirs." (CN I 95)

The powerful odors of the earth excite sexual drive in several instances. Philippe Cayol, in *Les Mystères de Marseille,* convinces Blanche de Cazalis to flee with him. At twilight, nature and the "evening's sensual pleasures" intervene to weaken the virginal resistance of Blanche in the arms of Philippe: "Des ombres transparentes tombaient du ciel pâle, et d'âcres odeurs montaient de la terre, chaude encore des derniers rayons." (6) These earth odors, among other strong factors, incite Laurent's passionate urge to possess the heroine of *Thérèse Raquin.* One Sunday Thérèse, Camille, and Laurent take their last excursion of the season to Saint-Ouen. Warm from walking in the sun, they look for a cool shady spot on one of the islands. They stretch out upon the earth and wait for the sunrays to weaken. Camille falls asleep. Laurent approaches Thérèse, who pretends to be asleep, and kisses her shoe. "Les senteurs âpres de la terre, les parfums légers de Thérèse se mêlaient et le pénétraient, en allumant son sang, en irritant ses nerfs." (64) Only the presence of her husband prevents Laurent from gratifying his desire in this otherwise ideal setting (64).

A strong odor in nature mixing with that of woman to spur on male desire occurs in *La Terre,* too. Françoise slides down from the top of a haystack into the arms of Jean, knocking him onto the earth. He grabs her in his arms. The odors from her body and the hay intoxicate him: "Cette odeur âcre de fille, ce parfum violent de foin fouetté de grand air, le grisaient, raidissaient tous ses muscles, dans une rage brusque de désir." (144) He releases his hold when she protests that he is hurting her. Jean realizes now that it is Françoise he wants, not her sister. As the earth odors intensify, the landscape subtly acquires a feminine aspect with the roundnesses of the haystacks, suggestive of breasts, silhouetted against the twilit sky (145). And it is during another hay harvest that Jean and Françoise are drawn closer together, and that he again entertains thoughts of seducing her as they sit in silence, enveloped in the darkness of night and the strong odor of hay perfuming the air (195).

In *La Faute de l'abbé Mouret,* aromatic plants arouse Serge's desire to possess Albine. In the sweltering heat, the couple investigate a rocky terrain. Spicy and pungent scents of aromatic plants intoxicate the lovers, and the resinous dust of dry pine needles, crushed under foot, burn their lips. A strange fever that invades their bodies momentarily subsides upon their arrival at some refreshing natural springs. But their anxiety returns, intensified, as they reach a plateau where overpowering odors of strong and foul-smelling plants assail them. Among the various herbs whose scents befuddle the pair are "la rue, d'une odeur de chair fétide; la valériane, brûlante, toute trempée de sa sueur aphrodisiaque" (228). Both feel faint. Serge, who realizes that their giddiness is caused by the odoriferous herbs, leads Albine to a shady spot to rest. She trembles at his very touch. The tree above them, with its highly polished greenery, is reptilian in appearance. "Là, sous ces ombrages lourds, la chaleur avait un sommeil voluptueux. L'air dormait, sans un souffle, dans une moiteur d'alcôve. Un parfum d'amour oriental, le parfum des lèvres peintes de la Sulamite, s'exhalait des bois odorants." (229) This 'voluptuous', humid heat serves a similar, if venal purpose, in *Nana*, whose heroine recognizes it as an accomplice of sexual desire, and, as a prostitute, exploits its aphrodisiac power. Business is especially fine on the hot humid nights of summer: "Les soirs humides, lorsque Paris mouillé exhalait une odeur fade de grande alcôve mal tenue, elle savait que ce temps mou, cette fétidité des coins louches enrageaient les hommes." (247)

Albine asks Serge if he is not going to sit down beside her. At a second bidding, he kneels several feet from her. He explains that were he any closer his fever would burn her. But very gradually he begins to approach her and confesses his desire to possess her. When he kisses the hem of her skirt, she suggests that they continue their walk. Next they come to a rocky area where thick-leaved plants resemble monstrous, malformed, naked-bellied spiders and bristly caterpillars, crouching and crawling about, somewhat like the fantasy-world monsters in a Hieronymus Bosch painting. Serge pleads that they return to the shade, but the spot they choose is speckled with sunlight. "L'astre y triomphait, y prenait la terre nue, la serrait contre l'embrasement de sa poitrine." (231) Albine now asks Serge to take her. They begin to caress each other frantically, but abruptly cease and flee along separate paths.

Following the idyllic interlude in the Paradou, Abbé Mouret discovers that he can no longer resume his customary long walks into the countryside. On two different mornings the priest starts off toward the country but cannot go beyond the village itself; "il était rentré, troublé par les odeurs, le plein soleil, la largeur de l'horizon" (219). He personally undertakes the manual labor to repair and beautify the church and thereby avoids and suppresses "le dehors, les arbres, le soleil, les vents tièdes qui le troublaient" (292). Fearful that Abbé Mouret might weaken to some temptation and consequently return to Albine, Frère Archangias maintains a constant vigil against the entry into the church of a direct ray of sunlight or the odor of any plant.

In *La Curée* the heady perfumes of tropical flora and the humid heat in the hothouse are especially instrumental in arousing Renée's latent incestuous desire. While standing in the hothouse, she jealously and surreptitiously observes her stepson Maxime chatting with Louise in the adjacent salon. Some plants metamorphose into animals, while others undergo partial anthropomorphosis. Similes stressing the sinister and sickly slither into and intertwine with the sensual and erotic images in the lengthy description of the overwhelming profusion of the multifold flora in the hothouse. The plants twist into snakes, flatten into toads, stiffen into swords and daggers, exhale an acrid breath, expose leprous or pimply exteriors, bleed, and exude poisons; the warped, strange, and monstrous mingle with voluptuously humid lips, sensual warmth, velvety softness and carnal reds of rose, crimson, and scarlet (44-46). The imagery of sensual mouths and exuding poisons suggests the imminent nascence of incestuous desire into Renée's consciousness. This desire, amorphous and nebulous in the cool Bois de Boulogne at twilight in the opening chapter of the novel, begins to crystalize clearly in the midst of the flaming, vapor-laden, fermenting atmosphere of the hothouse. "Un amour immense, un besoin de volupté, flottait dans cette nef close, où bouillait la sève ardente des tropiques. La jeune femme était prise dans ces noces puissantes de la terre.... A ses pieds, le bassin, la masse d'eau chaude ... fumait, mettait à ses épaules un manteau de vapeurs lourdes, une buée qui lui chauffait la peau, comme l'attouchement d'une main moite de volupté. Sur sa tête, elle sentait le jet des Palmiers, les hauts feuillages secouant leur arôme. ...c'étaient surtout les odeurs qui la brisaient." (47) The warm, voluptuous moisture, charged with natural scents suggesting human sweat, breath, and hair, and permeated with the contagiously pestilential and poisonous, invades and infects Renée's being.

Mais, dans cette musique étrange des odeurs, la phrase mélodique qui revenait toujours, dominant, étouffant les tendresses de la Vanille et les acuités des Orchidées, c'était cette odeur humaine, pénétrante, sensuelle, cette odeur d'amour qui s'échappe le matin de la chambre close de deux jeunes époux.

... A cette heure de vision nette, toutes ses bonnes résolutions s'évanouissaient à jamais.... Ses sens de femme ardente, ses caprices de femme blasée s'éveillaient. (47-48)

The next day Renée is remorseful for having entertained thoughts of committing incest with her husband's son. But after Maxime seduces her in a private dining room of the Café Riche, Renée seeks consciously to continue the incestuous relationship. Although Maxime prefers to make love to Renée in her bedroom where he finds her delightfully sensual, Renée prefers the greenhouse where she practically ravishes him. The intense humid heat and heavy air in the hothouse sap Maxime's energy, but activate Renée's. The entire hothouse seems simultaneously engaged in its own lovemaking. The palely lit, vaguely shaped leafy masses of the tropical plants evoke sensual images: roundnesses of hips, limbs embracing, caresses, hair, etc. The pair watch the long shoots of certain plants exchange amorous embraces. The vegetation transfers its heat of sexual desire to the lovers, while the steaming heat of the hothouse drips down on them from the palms overhead and rises into their bodies from the earth below. They feel the vital sap of the trees penetrate them and instill an immediate desire to grow and reproduce. The plants echo the couple's intimate sounds of passion: "...des murmures, des chuchotements leur venaient des massifs, voix pâmées, soupirs d'extase, cris étouffés de douleur, rires lointains, tout ce que leurs propres baisers avaient de bavard, et que l'écho leur renvoyait." (189) The earth itself seems to tremble in voluptuous excitement. But it is the odors which play the primary role: "S'ils avaient fermé les yeux, si la chaleur suffocante et la lumière pâle n'avaient pas mis en eux une dépravation de tous les sens, les odeurs eussent suffi à les jeter dans un éréthisme nerveux extraordinaire." (189)

4. CONCEALMENT

O forêts! Bois profonds! solitudes! asiles!

Hugo

Nature provides mystery and intimacy for lovers when its horizons close in around them. And physical rejuvenation often takes place then. Thickets are discreet guardians of the author and Ninon's love, in the Preface to the *Nouveaux Contes à Ninon*. The couple walk far from town into the "discreet darkness". "Il n'est pas de buisson qui n'ait caché nos baisers, étouffé nos causeries." (CN 274) In the short story "Les Fraises", the author reminisces over an excursion that he and Ninon took into the Verrières woods. In these 'discreet' woods, silent witnesses to their love, only the warblers and the thickets might see them kiss. Dark narrow paths squeeze them closer together. Dense thickets hide their amorous kissing (CN 298). As they penetrate the heart of the forest, they feel rejuvenated: "Le silence frissonnant, l'ombre vivante qui tombait des grands arbres nous montaient à la tête, nous grisaient de toute la sève ardente du printemps. On redevient enfant, dans le mystère des taillis." (CN 298)

"Mystery" and "silence" pervade another thick leafy passage and heighten a joyful mood in the short story "Les Voleurs et l'âne". The author notes that his companion Léon has succumbed youthfully to the morning beauty as they walk along a narrow path bordered with high hedges. "Les haies, hautes et touffues, étaient tout notre horizon. Cette sorte d'emprisonnement et l'ignorance où nous étions de la route, redoublaient notre gaîté." (CN 130) Zola reflects that he has always liked these narrow and spiny hedge-bordered paths for they not only impel physical contact for lovers, but also provide an intimate setting where only warblers can hear them kiss (CN 130). The narrowing path forces the men to walk in single file, but then allows Léon to gallantly cede passage to Antoinette, who approaches in the company of two young men. The two parties row out to an island in the single boat available. Antoinette claps her hands gleefully at the sight of the impenetrable green wall of tall trees, bushes, grass, and moss along the periphery of the island. Reflected in the water, the encircling wall of the bulwark-like structure appears doubly tall. The formidable exterior incites their curiosity to seek the mystery that may lie within. "Au dehors, un rempart de rameaux enlacés; au dedans, on ne savait. Cette ignorance des clairières, ce large rideau de verdure qui tremblait au vent, sans jamais s'écarter, faisait de l'île une retraite mystérieuse, que le passant des rives voisines peuplait volontiers des blanches filles de la rivière." (CN 136) The word *rideau* here hints at a theater curtain which, when drawn open, will unveil the setting and action behind. While Jeanne of *Le Vœu d'une morte* is staying at the Telliers' summer estate near the Seine, her curiosity is drawn to the river islands separated by narrow channels, like "discreet lanes" with their overhanging tree branches (94).

The newlyweds of the short story "Voyage circulaire" spend the last week of their honeymoon in a restful country setting, where, by day, their love is hidden by the verdure along the unfrequented paths (CN II 526). Sometimes, in *Madeleine Férat*, the heroine and Guillaume strike off along unknown, narrow country paths across the countryside, and are childishly gleeful if they meet no one along the way (100). On their first long cross-country walk, the view of a lonely, thickly wooded valley causes Madeleine to link her arm tightly into Guillaume's. "La fatigue, les voluptés des ombrages, le réveil de sa jeunesse, le lieu sauvage qu'elle traversait, tout mettait dans son être une émotion amoureuse, une de ces langueurs des sens qui font tomber aux bras d'un homme les femmes les plus fières." (12) The wild quality of the landscape gives off an air of mystery, while the absence of other human beings and the presence of voluptuous shadows offer intimacy.

In *La Faute de l'abbé Mouret*, the trees around the legendary one in the Paradou form an impenetrable leafy wall and dome, creating "un tabernacle de silence et de demi-jour.... Une langueur d'alcôve, ... Solitude nuptiale, ..." (251) In the presence of such surroundings, Serge and Albine gradually relax "au plaisir d'être ensemble, très loin, au fond d'une retraite miraculeusement cachée" (252).

In addition to the intimacy that nature can provide, the ideal natural settings for lovers contain the presence of some light to brighten the shadows or to filter basic darkness. The light from the moon is welcome when diffused or filtered. For example, in the above-named novel, the moon is 'discreet' because it watches Serge and Albine return home one night through the interstices of the leaves of the trees (224). On the other hand, direct moonlight is threatening for the young lovers in "Naïs Micoulin", because the moon witnesses their actions and may reveal their presence to some human observer (CN I 96). Consequently they seek darker surroundings, as do Jacques and Séverine of *La Bête humaine* on summer and fall nights. "Des cieux étoilés, des lunes éclatantes, les gênèrent; mais, à ces rendez-vous-là, ils filaient dans les raies d'ombre, ils cherchaient les coins d'obscurité, où il était si bon de se serrer l'un contre l'autre." (178)

The moon plays a more complex but decisive role in precipitating love between the two protagonists in the short story "Le Bain". Adeline, bathing in the nude late at night in the spring-fed pool beside the grotto, blushingly discovers that the young Count Octave de R... has already been in the water for some time. The moon is shining so brightly that she will not permit him to leave the pool, even were she to turn her back to him. The light from the stars intensifies that of the moon, making the water shockingly transparent; "cette diablesse de lune se baignait, elle aussi, se roulait dans l'eau, l'emplissait des frétillements d'anguilles de ses rayons" (CN 292). Adeline will permit the Count to leave the water only when the moon reaches a certain tree to place them in shadow. However, it is evident that the moon will dally for another hour before arriving there. Adeline partially covers herself with floating lily-pads. They discuss the weather. The Count reveals that he has loved her for two years. The dazzling moonbeams shine directly into her eyes, dizzying her. He speaks again of his love for her, but she asks him to be silent until the moon disappears. And the story concludes: "La lune se cacha derrière l'arbre. L'Amour de plâtre éclata de rire." (CN 294)

A sea grotto affords seclusion and semi-darkness to a couple in love, in "Les Coquillages de M. Chabre". A mounting tide isolates Estelle, the young wife of the middle-aged Chabre, and the youthful Hector, in a grotto. Hector pretends surprise and announces to Chabre on the cliff above that there will be a two-hour wait before they can rejoin him. Following Chabre's concern that his wife does not catch cold, Hector sits very near Estelle and soon takes her hand in his. As twilight falls, "l'eau entrait dans la grotte, roulant avec un bruit doux les graviers transparents. Elle y apportait les voluptés du large, une voix caressante, une odeur irritante, chargée de désirs." (CN I 248) Hector tells Estelle repeatedly that he loves her as night settles about the secluded lovers.

The sea appears metaphorically, and the light that filters the darkness is seen only inwardly, in a scene from *La Fortune des Rougon*. A predawn fog rising from the Viorne river so darkens the night that Silvère and Miette had to grope painstakingly up to a particular rock on a slope of the Garrigues. "Autour d'eux se creusait un abîme de ténèbres. Ils étaient comme perdus sur la pointe d'un récif, au-dessus du vide." (182) The "muted rumbling" of the passing army of insurgents from below suggests the distant roar of the ocean. The marine metaphors are exploited further when the couple feel as though "un flot les avait jetés sur le bord de la route et que la mer s'était ensuite retirée" (182). As Silvère and Miette embrace each other for warmth, "des lueurs passaient devant leurs paupières closes" (184). And thus some "light" filters through their darkness. They exchange their first real kiss and, realizing that the night was an "accomplice", quickly sit apart in embarrassed confusion (184).

In a flashback to their budding love as youngsters, Zola manipulates in a unique manner the basic elements employed in most of the foregoing natural settings. When Miette was only eleven years old and Silvère still an adolescent, they would meet on opposite sides of a wide well shared by their two families. They could not see each other, separated by the Jas-Meiffren wall which bisects the upper part of the well. Yet the water surface reflects Miette's image to Silvère and his to her, and it also echoes their spoken confidences to one another. The well possesses an enchanting aura of mystery that seems to transport the young couple to an intimate spot in nature. "En bas, dans un demi-jour mystérieux, des lueurs vertes couraient, qui paraissaient changer le trou humide en une cachette perdue au fond des taillis. Ils s'apercevaient ainsi dans une sorte de nid verdâtre, tapissé de mousse, au milieu de la fraîcheur de l'eau et du feuillage." (200) Strange sounds come from inside the well: "...travail sourd de l'humidité, soupirs de l'air, gouttes d'eau glissant sur les pierres et dont la chute avait la sonorité grave d'un sanglot." (200) This cool, humid retreat is especially welcome on hot midsummer mornings; "ils étaient au fond de leur cachette verte, sous la terre, dans ce trou mystérieux et vaguement effrayant" (201).

Although the outer structure prevents any direct sensory contact between them, the well mysteriously joins the young lovers together in its "discreet depths". It abets their romance: "Il y eut ainsi des drames et des comédies dont le puits fut complice. Ce bienheureux trou, avec ses glaces blanches et son écho musical, hâta singulièrement leur tendresse." (202) Their illusory seclusion at the bottom of the well materializes in novel fashion in another setting on rainy evenings. As they sit wrapped together in Miette's cloak inside a low shelter, they listen to the rain outside and happily enjoy their shared isolation, deepened by the sensation of being under water (216). The pleasant sensation of suspension psychoanalytically resembles that experienced by the prenatal being. Moreover, it is likely that the low shelter forces the seated figures into a fetal-like position. Also, in the earlier scenes, womb-like imagery can be imputed to both the actual well and the illusion it evoked for Silvère and Miette. Besides the protective and secluding walls of the well, the intimate darkness containing the vitality of some light, the soft undersurface of their fancied moss-lined 'nest' at the bottom of the well, there are also the slow moving waters in the form of drops of moisture that collect to slide down the walls and drip into the water below. The presence of slow moving waters, then, is a desired element in a setting for concealed lovers.

5. THE STREAM OF LOVE

> Une eau courait, fraîche et creuse,
> Sur les mousses de velours;
> Et la nature amoureuse
> Dormait dans les grands bois sourds.
>
> Hugo

The waters of a river, as observed in the subsection "Water", interrelate sensuously and erotically with the human being. More often they reveal themselves as another accomplice of love. Their proximate presence melds with the other voluptuous and intimate qualities of an ideal natural setting for lovers. The stream of love, whose waters may vary in volume from a river to a trickle, flows slowly through or near the setting which conceals lovers in nature.

The stream of love plays a strong role in advancing the love of Silvère and Miette in *La Fortune des Rougon*. For two summers the youngsters run about the countryside, climb trees, and engage in other childish activities in order to avoid the intoxicating scents of the plants in the Saint-Mittre impasse. But whenever they rest beside the Viorne river, the suffocating sensation returns. "Les creux de la Viorne, surtout, étaient pour eux pleine d'une ombre fiévreuse." (219) Their childlike gaiety disappears when they lie down together on the grass in the voluptuous, star-brightened shadows of the willows, and hear the waters lap gently like "wet lips" (219). Then Silvère and Miette feel giddy and embrace briefly, but invariably the boy senses the potential danger and suggests that they wade out to one of the islands.

Some evenings as they swim together, the trees that line the river banks appear especially intent on providing discreet intimacy: their leafy curtains seem mysteriously to "s'épaissir, se pencher vers eux, draper leur retraite de rideaux énormes" (221). The ghostly play of moonlight on and about the dark shapes along the river banks fascinates the girl. Some tree masses seem to lengthen as if to follow her. The noctural "sighs" from the hidden countryside beyond and the lapping of the waves along the banks intrigue her. The eerie visual and auditory sensations combine with the sensual caressing of the flowing waters to release an inexplicable emotion in Miette. At such times she keeps beyond Silvère's reach in the water and hides while changing clothes. "La rivière n'avait plus pour eux qu'une ivresse amollie, un engourdissement voluptueux, qui les troublait étrangement." (223)

Closely related to this river episode is a curious phenomenon that takes place on warm and dark September evenings when Silvère and Miette tread silently the thick, grassy path between the Jas-Meiffren wall and the plank piles. The two sides seem to change into river banks, and impart to the young couple the sensation of floating down a river. "Et, dans ce vague du sol qu'ils roulaient, dans cette ressemblance de l'allée à un ruisseau d'ombre coulant sous le ciel noir et or, ils éprouvaient une émotion indéfinissable, ils baissaient la voix, bien que personne ne pût les entendre. Se livrant à ces ondes silencieuses de la nuit, la chair et l'esprit flottants, ils se contaient, ces soirs-là, les mille riens de leur journée, avec des frissons d'amoureux." (37) But on clear nights when moonlight reveals the true identity of the lane, they become like playful children again; "il suffisait d'un peu d'ombre pour que leur étreinte fût plus douce et leur rire plus mollement voluptueux" (213).

The basic components of natural settings for lovers are somewhat modified for a first amorous encounter, in "Printemps" of "Les Quatre journées de Jean Gourdon". When the hero learns through his uncle that Babet loves him, he waits for her to pass by the rectory. A vague, soft, and muted quality permeates the nocturnal scene. A 'velvety' light pervades the night sky. A cool breeze wafts poignant odors. Though attenuated in one instance and in suggestive form in another, the element of water assumes its presence through the distant lapping sounds from the Viorne river and the following simile: "La vallée s'étendait comme une mer d'ombre, sans rivage, douce et transparente." (CN 436) Jean flusters Babet when he discloses what Lazare confided to him earlier in the day. She tries to leave, but Jean holds her hand in his. The two notice that they are in a natural enclosure, "a kind of hollow which the hedge formed" (CN 436). Soon they are seated there speaking of their love and plans for the future; "et toute la vallée chuchotant dans l'ombre, prenait plaisir à nous entendre causer si doucement" (CN 437).

A natural setting for lovers in *Au Bonheur des dames* is inauspicious for one couple, but ideal, were there a substitute for one of the parties. Denise accompanies a couple on a Sunday outing to Joinville. That evening, they dine at the restaurant on the island in the Marne river. Afterwards, Denise sees the shy Deloche outside and suggests that he escort her on a walk about the island. Leaving behind them the noisy crowd and suffocating heat of the restaurant, they penetrate the chilly, ever-darkening shadows of the trees beside the trickling waters of the river. Yet there is some light, for the treetops are "criblés d'étoiles tandis que, sur la droite, l'eau par moments avait dans le noir un luisant de miroir d'étain" (157). Deloche stammers out how glad he is to have met her here. "Et, les ténèbres aidant, après bien des paroles embarrassées, il osa dire qu'il l'aimait. Depuis longtemps, il voulait le lui écrire; et jamais elle ne l'aurait su peut-être, sans cette belle nuit complice, sans cette eau qui chantait et ces arbres qui les couvraient du rideau de leurs ombrages." (157) Denise does not answer. Instead, she begins to sob, thinking shamefully that had the popular Hutin been avowing love to her in this particular setting, she could not have resisted his advances.

In *Le Rêve* the 'milky' light of a veiled moon permeates the dreamlike scene of the lovers' idyllic promenade beside languidly flowing waters, to enhance the overall ethereality and impart a quality of purity and innocence to the lovers. Illumined by the lacteous light of the moon, Félicien leads Angélique into his father's vast garden, the Clos-Marie. "Au ciel, la lune peu à peu montante, cachée derrière le voile de vapeurs chaudes, les blanchissait d'une transparence laiteuse. Toute la voûte, sans une étoile, en était emplie d'une poussière de clarté, qui pleuvait muette dans la sérénité de la nuit." (132). Reality seems to merge into illusion as the setting and action gradually acquire the dimensions of a dream. In the liquescent atmosphere of this 'dream' within the more vast dream of *Le Rêve*, movement slackens into flowing slow motion while unsubstantial objects of blurred shapes float in suspension. Even the waters of the Chevrotte which rush further downstream are relaxed here, "une eau calme, une eau alanguie, errant parmi des touffes d'arbres. Et, sous la nuée lumineuse, entre ces arbres baignés et flottants, la rivière élyséenne semblait se dérouler dans un rêve." (132) Furthermore, the softness of the surface upon which the lovers walk (134) hints at the sensation of floating or being in suspension.

Though diffused, the brighter light of the sun guards the childlike purity of Serge and Albine's burgeoning love in *La Faute de l'abbé Mouret*. Following a river downstream, the couple comes to a pleasant spot where three willows stand at the edge of the water. Beneath the "tent of greenery" formed by the willows, Serge and Albine pretend like innocent children to be husband and wife at work in their home. Eventually they lie down beside one another. To conserve the innocence of this particular phase of their romantic relationship, the author modifies accordingly the basic elements found in other ideal settings in nature for lovers:

C'était l'amour avant le sexe, ... Autour d'eux, les prairies largement ouvertes les rassuraient de la légère peur qu'ils avaient l'un de l'autre. Ils se savaient vus de toutes les herbes, vus du ciel dont le bleu les regardait à travers le feuillage grêle; et cela ne les dérangeait pas.... L'ombre restait si claire, qu'elle ne leur soufflait pas les langueurs des taillis profonds, les sollicitations des trous perdus, des alcôves vertes. Du bout de l'horizon, leur venait un air libre, un vent de santé, apportant la fraîcheur de cette mer de verdure, où il soulevait une houle de fleurs; tandis que, à leurs pieds, la rivière était une enfance de plus, une candeur dont le filet de voix fraîche leur semblait la voix lointaine de quelque camarade qui riait.... Immense champ, au milieu duquel le gazon étroit qui leur servait de première couche, prenait une naïveté de berceau. (211)

Instead of providing the intimate seclusion of impenetrable or thickly foliaged walls, the thin curtains of this tent let in light and open out onto an expansive horizon. Although a wind wafts over the flowers, it is sufficiently brisk to prevent any amassing of tantalizing scents. The laughing waters of the stream do not change into slow flowing waters, as did those of the Chevrotte in the description quoted from *Le Rêve*. There-fore, by implying the absence of certain elements, the author intimates how nature can abet a more sensual love. As their love progresses the couple will seek greater womb-like security, as exemplified in their later wishes that the prairie grasses were "plus grandes qu'eux, afin de se perdre dans leur flot mourant, d'être plus seuls, d'être loin de tout" (373-374).

Only a thin trickle of water runs through the thickly shaded setting that secludes the lovers in *Le Docteur Pascal*. La Souléiade is enclosed by walls to prevent the entry of any disturbing element from the world outside. Pascal and Clotilde enjoy their strolls about the terraced plantings of olive and almond trees, in the resin-scented pine grove, but most of all in the thick shade of the grove of plane trees. There they can wander in and around the labyrinth formed by the big boxwood shrubs. They listen blissfully to the trickling water of the fountain in this shadowy retreat. "Ils restaient assis près du bassin moussu, ils laissaient tomber là le cré-puscule, peu à peu noyés sous les ténèbres des arbres, les mains unies, les lèvres rejointes, tandis que l'eau, qu'on ne voyait plus filait sans fin sa note de flûte." (177)

Trickling waters dwindle to falling drops. In *Madeleine Férat*, the heroine and Guillaume's favorite natural setting is a grassy clearing, sur-rounded by an "impenetrable wall" of rushes and high brushwood, beside a small stream-fed lake. Because of a natural spring there, they name the site La Source. Here they are lulled by the drops of water dripping from the spring in the nearby grotto; "il y avait dans ce bruit un bercement sans fin, une sensation vague de sommeil et d'éternité qui plaisaient à leurs amours heureuses. Peu à peu, ils cessaient de parler, gagnés par la monotonie de la chanson continue des gouttes d'eau, croyant entendre les battements de leur cœur, rêvant et souriant, la main dans la main." (99) Psychoanalytically, the steady pulsating sound of the dripping water is like the reassuring heartbeat of the expectant mother for the fetal being.

Once again the imagery throughout contains the usual elements of the high protective wall encircling and secluding the lovers, the surface soft-ness, the light filtering the deep shadows, and the slow moving waters. The emphasis upon the pleasant sensation of being lulled reinforces the premise that these natural settings for lovers suggest, perhaps uncon-sciously for both author and participants, womb-like security and con-tentment.

6. GENERAL REMARKS

Le crépuscule ami s'endort dans la vallée
Sur l'herbe d'émeraude et sur l'or du gazon,
Sous les timides joncs de la source isolée
Et sous le bois rêveur qui tremble à l'horizon
Se balance en fuyant dans les grappes sauvages,
Jette son manteau gris sur le bord des rivages,
Et des fleurs de la nuit entr'ouvre la prison.

Vigny

Nature, an accomplice of love, participates in love by presenting varied patterns of certain essential elements. Restricted horizons provide intimacy for lovers. Open, immense panoramas tend to cause man to reflect upon his human condition in relation with the universe; and melancholy ensues. A pensive and anguished meditation isolates him, even in the company of his beloved. Thus, expansive vistas can separate lovers. Conversely, horizons that press in closely impel physical contact of man and woman. Also, they insulate the couple as a unit from the rest of the universe. Spontaneous, youthful exuberance and joy consequently spring forth. Thick leafy walls hide lovers from the gaze of the outside world. These green curtains seem cloaked in mystery which, in turn, heightens the romantic mood. Part of that mystery resides in the unconscious suggestiveness of womb-like seclusion and security. Impenetrable walls of greenery surround and enclose lovers on a horizontal plane, while on a vertical one trees stretch their protective branches above them. Milky diffused moonlight or even bright sunlight sifts through leafy vaults to the couple below. Or if they are in a clearing, flickering stars filter the blackness of night. Shadows deepen for the nonnocturnal scene. But in all cases the presence of some vital light brightens basic darkness. Rays or reflections of light enter even the domed enclosure of a sea grotto. Soft surfaces of grass or moss impart a sensation of suspension or floating. Water itself is a prime and ever-present element. Most often it takes the form of a stream flowing slowly nearby. The languidly flowing waters reinforce the uterine imagery by suggesting the liquid that surrounds the fetal sac or even the vaginal track that leads to the womb. By extension, then, the vaginal aspect may explain part of the 'mystery' attributed to the high hedge-bordered paths and the tree-lined lanes. Furthermore, echoes from prenatal existence beat reasuringly in the steady rhythmic sounds from flowing, lapping, trickling or dripping waters of these streams of love. These and other vague 'voices' in nature often release the preconscious thought or sentiment into the consciousness.

The auditory sense is the most suggestive of the five physical senses for lovers who find themselves in natural settings. But nature arouses and plays upon the other senses as well. Nature echoes back, stronger and louder, the feelings and emotions that lovers invest in it. Consequently, nature often appears to anthropomorphize for them. Or for the one not yet in love but ready for the experience, and prior to instigating and advancing love between the latter and another human being, nature may assume anthropomorphic guise in order to establish a preliminary sensual or erotic relationship with the individual person. The visual sense, in particular, endows nature with human form. Man transfers the sinuous lines, fleshy tones, and carnal reds of nature into sensual images of woman. Vague shapes of plants viewed in semi-darkness metamorphose into seductive female flesh and form. The tactile sense bares its sensitivity to the warm caresses of sunlight or the cool voluptuousness of shadows or waters. The gustatory sense, the least often recorded by Zola, functions generally in synesthetic confusion with the olfactory, and then, usually to identify the acridity or sweetness of odors. This is best exemplified in the passage of *La Faute de l'abbé Mouret* where the spring morning awakens in turn each of the five senses of the convalescing Serge: "Il le goûtait venir, d'une saveur de plus en plus nette, lui apportant l'amertume saine du grand air, mettant à ses lèvres le régal des aromates sucrés, des fruits acides, des bois laiteux." (164-165) Lovers in nuptial settings invest the intangible scents of nature with human odors. Generally, the olfactory is the most powerful of the five senses to precipitate seduction.

But if man's senses fail, nature loses its power as an accomplice of love. This is the case when Serge, a priest once again, returns to the Paradou. He is depressed by the autumnal scene. Neither nature nor Albine can restimulate his senses. In desperation, Albine leads him back to the site of the legendary tree. The park renews its former efforts at complicity in love:

Comme au jour de leurs noces, une langueur d'alcôve, une lueur de nuit d'été mourant sur l'épaule nue d'une amoureuse, un balbutiement d'amour à peine distinct, tombant brusquement à un grand spasme muet, traînaient dans la clairière, baignée d'une limpidité verdâtre. Et, au loin, le Paradou, malgré le premier frisson de l'automne, retrouvait, lui aussi, ses chuchotements ardents. Il redevenait complice. Du parterre, du verger, des prairies, de la forêt, des grandes roches, du vaste ciel, arrivait de nouveau un rire de volupté, un vent qui semait sur son passage une poussière de fécondation. Jamais le jardin, aux plus tièdes soirées de printemps, n'avait des tendresses si profondes qu'aux derniers beaux jours, lorsque les plantes s'endormaient en se disant adieu. L'odeur des germes mûrs charriait une ivresse de désir, à travers les feuilles plus rares. (379-380)

Albine pleads with Serge to listen to the Paradou which implores them to love each other. Serge only cries. Unable to resuscitate his desire with her kisses, she drives him out of the garden and returns alone into it. "La nuit tombait, le jardin n'était plus qu'un grand cercueil d'ombre." (380) Mother Nature cannot seclude in her womb anyone for whom love is dead.

VI

PATHETIC FALLACY

> Et quelque chose en moi, comme dans la nature,
> Pleurait, priait, souffrait, bénissait tour à tour!
>
> Lamartine

Pathetic fallacy, deplored by Ruskin,[1] is a device commonly employed by the romantic.[2] Zola, the 'naturalist', also attributes human traits and feelings to nature and inanimate objects. Zola uses pathetic fallacy richly and with great variety to enhance man's personality or state of being. Nature reflects his feelings, mirrors his emotions, magnifies his passion. Or, conversely, it placidly ignores his sufferings. It prophesies his imminent tragedy. It struggles against him and menaces his life. And it optimistically offers him entry into its universal soul. Thus, Zola's manipulation of this poetic device offers five distinct principal varieties of pathetic fallacy which we are classifying accordingly as 'sympathetic and empathetic', 'apathetic', 'prophetic', 'malevolent', and finally 'benevolent'.

[1] See John Ruskin, *Modern Painters*, Vol. III, Part IV, in *The Works of John Ruskin*, eds. E. T. Cook and Alexander Wedderburn, Vol. V (London: George Allen, 1904), pp. 201-220. In a chapter entitled "Of The Prophetic Fallacy", Ruskin contrasts our ordinary perception of things with "the extraordinary, or false appearances, when we are under the influence of emotion, or contemplative fancy; false appearances, I say, as being entirely unconnected with any real power or character in the object, and only imputed to it by us". He illustrates this with two lines of verse from Oliver Wendell Holmes: "The spendthrift crocus, bursting through the mould / Naked and shivering, with his cup of gold." The critic then points out: "The crocus is not a spendthrift, but a hardy plant; its yellow is not gold, but saffron." (204) Similarly for Kingsley's line of poetry, "The cruel, crawling foam" from *Alton Locke*, Ruskin states, "The foam is not cruel, neither does it crawl." (205)
[2] See, for example, Josephine Miles, "Pathetic Fallacy in the Nineteenth Century", *University of California Publications in English* (Los Angeles, 1942), Vol. 12, No. 2, pp. vi and 183-304.

1. SYMPATHETIC AND EMPATHETIC FALLACY

Beau ciel tout sympathique, et tout peuplé d'échos!

Musset

Nature 'sympathizes' and even 'empathizes' with man when it appears to reflect his feelings and emotions. Since Zola employs sympathetic and empathetic fallacy so profusely throughout his works, and since most readers of literature, especially romantic, are well acquainted with this most obvious kind of pathetic fallacy, the relatively few examples presented here are selected primarily to indicate the rich gamut of variations. However, a thematic instance selected from one novel will be developed to illustrate the importance and continuity of this novelistic device in Zola's works.

Frequently, especially in the earlier works, the characters themselves consciously bestow their personal feelings on nature. In fact, one country-side acquires, Janus-like, two opposing faces in the course of a single day for one character in *Les Mystères de Marseille*. Filled with the hope of raising the funds necessary to purchase the freedom of his brother from prison, Marius brightens with "joyful gleams" the fields and hills on the morning trip by coach. However, during the sad and painful return after his unsuccessful attempt, he projects his anxiety upon that same country-side, "et Marius trouvait dans chaque nouveau paysage un deuil plus noir, une douleur plus poignante. La nuit vint, il lui sembla que le pays entier était couvert d'un crêpe immense." (102)

Blanche, the pale heroine of the same novel, separated from her lover, finds her tearful existence reflected in the melancholy and cold of autumn: "De larges frissons secouaient la mer dont les voix se faisaient gémissantes, tandis que les arbres jetaient leurs feuilles à la terre. Sous la nudité morne du ciel s'étalait la nudité des eaux et du rivage. Cette tristesse de l'air, ces derniers adieux de l'été mettaient autour de Blanche la désespérance qui était dans son cœur." (207)

The author may symbolically identify a seasonal change in nature with a turning point in his own life or that of a character. In true romantic tradition, autumnal melancholy sets a somber mood for the separation of lovers in the Preface to the *Contes à Ninon*. The young author, feeling that he has evaded long enough the harsh realities of the outside world, decides to sever his dreamlike existence with his fictitious Ninon in the midst of nature. He compares his uncertain future to the "unknown dawn" that will follow this mournful fall of night with its menace of fog, and he notes that the countryside is "moribund", like the girl who haunts his conscious dreams (CN 56-57).

Exceptionally, in "Les Quatre journées de Jean Gourdon", fall does not suggest melancholy and desolation. The four "days" fall on succeeding seasons of the year and comparable stages in the protagonist's life. "Automne", the third 'day', stresses twofold fecundity: Jean's bountiful harvest of grain and fruit; his wife's full bloom of maturity as she bears a son to him. Even though the shivering clouds, pale sky, black earth and wrinkling river hint of winter and death, the primary stress lies on golden richness and fecund nature:

De petits nuages blancs frissonnaient dans le ciel pâle. Le soleil avait des rayons blonds qui jetaient comme une poussière d'or sur la campagne, dont la nappe jaune s'étendait toute mûre, n'ayant plus les lumières ni les ombres énergiques de l'été. Les feuillages doraient par larges plaques, la terre noire. La rivière coulait plus lente, la vallée restait calme et forte. Elle portait déjà les premières rides de l'hiver, mais son flanc gardait la chaleur de ses derniers enfantements, étalant ses formes amples, dépouillées des herbes folles du printemps, plus orgueilleuse- ment belle de cette seconde jeunesse de la femme qui a fait œuvre de vie. (NCN 451)

Most often, Zola will describe how nature reflects the emotions of man, rather than allow man himself to transfer his feelings to the natural scene. This technique is often less subtle in the earlier short stories. For example, the sun beams in direct proportion to the happiness of Marthe, the young milliner of "L'Amour sous les toits", one of the "Esquissess parisiennes". The author compares her to a lark, whose "nest" is a garret. "Elle est l'âme de cet univers, et, selon qu'elle rit ou qu'elle pleure, le soleil entre ou n'entre pas." (CN I 34) In the "Aventures du grand Sidoine et du petit Médéric", the sun shines more brightly than usual on the day of the compassionate Primevère's birth. This princess has a literary sister in the charitable heroine of the short story "La Légende du Petit-Manteau bleu de l'Amour", on whose day of birth nature performs far more miracu- lously. Through a lightly falling December snow, foretokens of the girl's future mission of love appear in the rose-tinted rays from the early morn- ing sun upon the "virginal" snow, in the extraordinary wafting of lilac fragrance through the air, and in the springtime songs of birds (CN 351).

A joyful nature often smiles and laughs at dawn, in spring and in sum- mer. It mirrors the childish excitement of Serge and Albine, in *La Faute de l'abbé Mouret*, during their first venture together into the Paradou. The rosy morning "smiles" like an awakening infant (197). "Smiles" break into "laughter" in the long-abandoned fruit orchard. Climbing vines spring about the "smiling" peach trees and burst into wild "laughter".

The joy of nature is highly contagious, even along the paths, "tant les haies laissaient tomber de rires gourmands. Le parc avait, dans cet heureux verger, une gaminerie de buissons s'en allant à la débandade.... Rien de troublant ne leur venait du bois en récréation." (204) In the meadows they walk among rejoicing flowers (207). On their homeward trek they wade in a "laughing" stream, "playful like themselves" (212). "Retour charmant ... égayé de la belle humeur des eaux vivantes." (212-213)

The riotous flames of love often flare up in meridional settings. The passionate month-long courtship of Frédéric Rostand and the heroine of "Naïs Micoulin" takes place in an equally passionate "country of flames". Between the sea and the savage gorges behind the village of Estaque, just outside Marseilles, there is a stretch of red earth deeply quarried by tileworks "et dont une haleine d'ardente passion semble avoir séché les sources" (CN I 95). Gray and russet colors and the crackling sounds of active grasshoppers suggest the burning embers of this 'flaming' setting: "Le long des murailles, qui jettent des réverbérations de four, de petits lézards gris dorment, tandis que, du brasier des herbes roussies, des nuées de sauterelles s'envolent, avec un crépitement d'étincelles." (CN I 95)

But nature can be equally eloquent about misery and despair. A desolate landscape, monotonously cut up by small valleys and hills, reflects the tortured half-crazed mind of Jacques, in *La Bête humaine*, who has just run away from the temptation to kill Flore: "Ce pays désert, coupé de monticules, était comme un labyrinthe sans issue, où tournait sa folie, dans la morne désolation des terrains incultes." (55)

A muddy landscape that freezes over mirrors the death convulsions of Guillaume's love for the heroine of *Madeleine Férat*. The revelation of her past relationship with Jacques poisons Guillaume's love for her. The seeming defilement of their love extends its sullied tentacles throughout the house and about the muddy countryside, tainting and infecting everything in view. As the dropping temperature hardens the mud, the couple's own relationship petrifies, eventually becoming like the hard-frozen countryside across which the pair take flight in their two-seater gig. The moon sheds a steel-blue cast upon the icy plots of land. "Surpris au milieu du dégel, ils paraissaient s'être roidis pendant les secousses suprêmes de l'ouragan; ils avaient des arêtes aiguës, des flots de boue figée, des rigidités de cadavre glacé par la mort dans les dernières convulsions de l'agonie." (177) The analogy reappears as Madeleine "apercevait la campagne rigide et glacée qui s'allongeait avec des sécheresses de cadavre sous le suaire blanc de la lune" (181-182).

Winter loudly sounds the voice of misery and despair in the opening pages of *Germinal*. As Etienne strikes up a conversation with Bonnemort near Montsou, "le vent redoublait, une bise glaciale, dont les grandes haleines régulières passaient comme des coups de faux" (11). The old man relates how life has become increasingly difficult for the miners. The wintry wind howls the lament of the miners' miseries which seem to fill the shadows throughout the limitless countryside. "N'était-ce pas un cri de famine que roulait le vent de mars, au revers de cette campagne nue? Les rafales s'étaient enragées, elles semblaient apporter la mort du travail, une disette, qui tuerait beaucoup d'hommes." (13) During a lull in the conversation, "le vent passait avec sa plainte, comme un cri de faim et de lassitude venu des profondeurs de la nuit" (16). The icy gusts punctuate the old man's efforts to dissuade Etienne from seeking employment at the Voreux mine: "A chaque bourrasque, le vent paraissait grandir, comme s'il eût soufflé d'un horizon sans cesse élargi. Aucune aube ne blanchissait dans le ciel mort." (18) The gardens, too, serve to underscore the miserable living conditions. In contrast with the opulent estate of the Grégoires, whose fruit orchard and vegetable garden are renowned throughout the countryside, there are the row houses of the miners, whose pitifully small gardens, "ravagés par l'hiver, étalaient la tristesse de leur terre marneuse, que bossuaient et salissaient les derniers légumes" (105).

Gardens very often provide a bit of nature for those novels whose action takes place within the confines of a city. A garden in *L'Argent* reflects the genteel poverty of a countess. Mme Caroline's only distraction during a period of great sadness is to look down into the Countess of Beauvilliers' neighboring garden where she senses the existence of a fellow sufferer: "Les quelques beaux arbres du jardin restaient là comme au fond d'un puits, la mousse mangeait les marches du perron, émietté et fendu. On eût dit un coin de nature mis en prison, un coin doux et morne, d'une muette désespérance, où le soleil ne descendait plus qu'en un jour verdâtre, dont le frisson glaçait les épaules." (69)

A garden, the seasons, and the weather that alter the visage of Paris, faithfully mirror and punctuate changing nuances in the love of Hélène Grandjean for Henri Deberle, in *Une Page d'amour*. Zola deliberately makes sympathetic fallacy a central quality of this novel. In a letter-preface for the illustrated deluxe edition of 1884, he writes that, during his youthful years spent in various suburban garrets, he could look out a window, and always see Paris there, "comme le confident tragique de mes joies et de mes tristesses. J'ai eu faim et j'ai pleuré devant lui; et devant lui, j'ai aimé, j'ai eu mes plus grands bonheurs. Eh bien! dès ma vingtième année, j'avais rêvé d'écrire un roman dont Paris, avec l'océan de ses toitures, serait un personnage, quelque chose comme le chœur antique." (355)

Although the heroine's "confidant" is to be Paris, too, the natural phenomena there are of prime importance, in that a snow coldly whitens, a morning sun warmly yellows, and a setting sun ardently reddens the cityscape, while a driving downpour drowns and obscures, a fog hides, a mist veils and a sun unveils chosen monuments or entire sections of the city to reflect the evolving phases of Hélène's love. A review of certain highlights in two scenes from the first two sections, which depict that love from its awakening tenderness to its blossoming into passionate desire, evidences sympathetic fallacy as an integral part of both plot and structure.

Before the couple's first encounter and while Hélène seeks the help of a doctor for her ailing daughter, an icy wind blows over freshly fallen snow. This is like the painter's virginal canvas, the writer's white sheet of paper, the heroine's blank 'page of love'. Hélène engages the services of a Dr. Deberle who spends the night at the child's bedside. The "soft and gray light" of day dawning on the snow establishes a neutral background for the story of love to follow (17).

Then, in the garden scene where Hélène and Jeanne call upon the doctor's wife on the first beautiful day in February, nature timidly makes its appearance in thin, pale pastel washes through a fine, falling spray of sunshine and a light, floating ground mist: "Ce jour-là, dans le ciel pâle, le soleil mettait une poussière de lumière blonde. C'était, entre les branches sans feuilles, une pluie lente de rayons. Les arbres rougissaient, on voyait les fins bourgeons violâtres attendrir le ton gris de l'écorce. Et sur la pelouse, le long des allées, les herbes et les graviers avaient des pointes de clarté, qu'une brume légère, au ras du sol, noyait et fondait. Il n'y avait pas une fleur, la gaîté seule du soleil sur la terre nue annonçait le printemps." (48) The delicate rendering of hues, depicting the first vernal blush of nature, foretells, at the same time, the springtime of Hélène's love for Henri. Urged on by Jeanne's entreaties, Hélène swings ever higher on the garden swing; but perceiving Henri's eyes upon her, she urges Rambaud in vain to stop the swing and, without warning, jumps suddenly out of it, spraining her knee. She will not allow the doctor to examine it; and seeing her blush, he respects her wish. Thus, the garden description is the artist's prepared ground for this delicate situation of budding subtle sentiments. Although no leaf, blade of grass or flower has yet appeared, the first hints of burgeoning tender life are now present.

The author expands these same qualities of vagueness, blurred shapes,

and attenuated colors into a long, lyrical descriptive passage of the shifting mists which, revealing and concealing different parts of Paris, portray
the mind and heart of the heroine as she only half perceives the inchoate
love that begins to stir within her (61-71). Subsequently, the abrupt
weather changes of this precocious spring reflect the early vicissitudes of
her slowly shaping love.

Then, one rainy afternoon, Hélène accompanies her daughter to a
children's costume party at the Deberles'. The shutters are closed and the
curtains drawn to keep out the gloomy light of outdoors, but at one
point, the salon door is left wide open. The sudden entry of dismal daylight darkens the dazzling light of lamps and candles inside. In like manner, Henri's blunt and repeated declarations of love for Hélène crudely
dull the luster of her platonic romance. She escapes into another room
where she is "blinded" by the light flooding in from outside. Afraid to
return to the salon, she dashes back to her own apartment, and, breathless, flings open a window onto a Paris where it is no longer raining.

Reversing his earlier technique of soft washes on white, absorbent
watercolor paper, the author now chooses to work on a black surface
upon which he rapidly moves from somber darks to bold daubs of increasingly brighter, hotter hues.

On the "ink-black" screen of her closed eyelids, Hélène reviews the
events of her sentimental relationship with Henri. When she opens her
eyes, the city is cast in slate blue-gray, the Seine in tarnished silver. Glim-
mers of light appear only in the gilding on the dome of the Invalides, but
"l'on eût dit des lampes allumées en plein jour, d'une mélancolie rêveuse
au milieu du deuil crépusculaire qui drapait la cité' (130). This dull daylight illumination that deadens the brilliance of artificial lights is, on a
grander scale, a variation of the earlier episode at the party. The lusterless,
soot-blackened buildings of the cityscape, "like a colossal and delicate
charcoal drawing", remind Hélène that she does not now, nor ever will
know Henri. While she struggles with her own emotions, the rays of the
sun launch an attack upon Paris. One "darts" between two clouds to gild
the towers of Notre-Dame, others "strike" the city, which begins to
brighten under the *coups de soleil*. The lowering sun "cracks" the clouds.
Gliding black masses of cloud shadows draw up in "battle array".

When sunrays burst and disperse like lingering fireworks over the
Champs-Elysées, Hélène suddenly realizes that she can no longer resist
Henri's advances. As she decides to abandon her scruples of the past, the
sun thrusts aside the last clouds; and, as it sets, its rays seem to set fire to
all of Paris. Warm golds, yellows, and oranges ignite pedestrians and

passing vehicles; flesh colors tint the chimneys and their smoke. Zola, the great defender of the Impressionist painters, seems intent on rivaling them in art as he adapts their techniques to his own medium of written expression. The passion which Hélène now acknowledges and approves within herself is reflected in nature through the ardent reds of the solar conflagration that transform the towers of Notre-Dame into flaming torches and other monuments into blazing bonfires. Showers of sparks spread into the outlying areas and quickly consume them in flames. Paris is turned into a monumental fiery furnace. "Hélène, baignée par ces flammes, se livrant à cette passion qui la consumait, regardait flamber Paris." (134-135)

However, just preceding this last quotation, there is the brief notation of clouds "bleeding" above the city, an omen, perhaps, that her love is ill-fated, underscored in the final descriptive passage of Paris where the city is crystallized in ice and buried under the snow of winter.

2. APATHETIC FALLACY

> Vivez, froide Nature, et revivez sans cesse
> Sous nos pieds, sur nos fronts, puisque c'est votre loi;
> Vivez et dédaignez, si vous êtes déesse,
> L'homme, humble passager, qui dut vous être un Roi.

Vigny

Nature, then, mirrors not only the emotions and feelings of man, but also sympathetically aids and encourages him, or even empathetically suffers with him in his misery and despair. But the reverse is another aspect of pathetic fallacy: a nature lofty, impassive, and indifferent to the condition of man. Pathetic fallacy, used — at times worn through with overuse — by the romantics, was reversed dramatically by Musset and Hugo, Zola's favorite poets in his youth. Vigny had proclaimed the indifference and hostility of nature in "La Maison du berger": "La nature se rit des souffrances humaines." But, perhaps, the strongest point of departure for this reversal of technique for Zola comes from a letter that he received from Flaubert, his realist master. In relating his visit to a leper colony in Algeria, Flaubert describes one of the patients, who must have served in part as a model for the blind man in *Madame Bovary*, painfully dragging himself to a fountain to drink: "Sa bouche, dont les lèvres étaient enlevées comme pour une brûlure, laissait voir le fond de son gosier. Il râlait en tendant vers nous ses lambeaux de chairs livides. Et la nature calme tout à l'entour!"[3] The last elliptical sentence, and particularly its exclamation mark, dramatically illustrates how nature displays its apathy.

To heighten the horrors of war, Zola frequently employs apathetic fallacy.[4] He interjects references to the serenity and beauty in nature when man slaughters man on the battlefield. "Été", the second section of "Les Quatre journées de Jean Gourdon", describes a battle between the French and the Austrians. The beauty of the summer day and the pure sky contrast tragically with the slaughter on the chalky plain: "O la splendide matinée, et quelle plaine stérile pour tuer et mourir!" (CN 442) Jean is wounded in the shoulder and struck to the ground. The vast white plain about him "étalait sa désolation sous la sérénité ardente du ciel" (CN 443). He manages to crawl to the side of his colonel. Each with one good arm helps the other to rise. In the rose-tinted rays of the setting sun, they stumble like drunken men across the battlefield in search of an ambulance. "C'était la fin d'un beau jour." (CN 447) The action for the short story "L'Attaque du moulin" is situated in the most "adorable" natural setting, which resembles an "enchanted park", in Lorraine. The story begins with a betrothal feast. "Jamais une paix plus large n'était descendue sur un coin plus heureux de nature." (CN II 340) Exactly one month later, while the sun rises "gaily" over this setting, a bloody battle ensues.

The use of apathetic fallacy is particularly effective in *La Débâcle*. Nature, at first, appears to empathize with the French when, above a military encampment near Mulhouse, an "anxious" stormy sky and "anxiety-charged" gusts of wind herald the disastrous news of the defeat of the French army at Froeschwiller (10). Night, heavily laden with some nameless horror, falls like a blanket of despair upon the soldiers' camp (26). However, the black news of Mac-Mahon's defeat begins to spread about the camp before dawn. "Une aube de deuil se levait, parmi les brumes couleur de suie qui étaient montées, là-bas, du fleuve lointain." (28) But at Mulhouse, the sun shines brightly: "Ce beau dimanche d'effroyable désastre avait sa gaîté, son ciel éclatant des jours de fête." (29)

The imminent battle at Sedan threatens to be postponed by a heavy morning fog; but, then, "le soleil se levait, les vapeurs de la Meuse s'envolèrent en lambeaux de fine mousseline, le ciel bleu apparut, se dégagea,

---

[3] Gustave Flaubert, *Correspondance* (Paris: Conard, 1910-12), II, p. 241.
[4] Not to be confused with Toynbee's definition of apathetic fallacy: "We now fall victims to the inverse 'Apathetic Fallacy' of treating living creatures as though they were inanimate." Arnold J. Toynbee, *A Study of History* (London: Oxford University Press, 1934), I, p. 8.

d'une limpidité sans tache. C'était l'exquise matinée d'une admirable journée d'été." (197) This dramatic lifting of the fog is described in more literally theatrical imagery when the scene shifts from Bazeilles to the Plateau d'Algérie to depict "le déroulement d'un décor, derrière le flottant rideau qui remontait avec lenteur vers les frises. Un clair ruissellement de soleil tombait du ciel bleu." (224) Earlier, amid artillery bursts, the Prussian troops were seen advancing across the "eternal and smiling nature" (213). Shortly before the sun sets in its rosy light, the Prussian king looks down over the vast valley bathed in a limpid golden light. Without remorse the victor scans below him the thousands of seemingly tiny cadavers strewn across "cette vallée immense où les incendies de Bazeilles, les massacres d'Illy, les angoisses de Sedan, n'empêchaient pas l'impassible nature d'être belle, à cette fin sereine d'un beau jour" (337).

Apathetic fallacy recurs throughout this novel, not only when the French and Prussian forces wage war, but also when the French battle against one another. Maurice and Jean witness one hungry comrade in arms plunge a knife into the throat of a fellow soldier for part of a loaf of bread, and then see him sit calmly beside his victim to devour the blood-speckled bread beneath a "beautiful starry sky" (432). This incident preludes the civil war waged by the Commune within the capital city. Paris begins its self-destruction by fire on a beautiful spring night. Hostages fall before the firing squad of the Commune. "Et Paris ensoleillé, endimanché, paraissait en fête." (583)

The death of the individual soldier loses all significance when it occurs in a totally impassive nature. As a small band of French troops retreat through a wood, heavily barraged by Prussian artillery, the flag bearer falls, a bullet in his lungs. He calls out for someone to save the flag while he remains alone, writhing in pain, "dans ce coin délicieux du bois" (344). Lieutenant Rochas takes the French flag, is shot in turn, crumples up, completely entangled in the battered flag, and lives one minute more. "Puis, il eut un petit hoquet, il s'en alla dans son ahurissement d'enfant, tel qu'un pauvre être borné, un insecte joyeux, écrasé sous la nécessité de l'énorme et impassible nature." (356)

The insignificance of man in the midst of an "enormous and impassive nature" becomes more poignant when he is thus compared and reduced in stature to a mere insect. This image appears in other works. The peasants who work in the fields are often compared to "insects" and "ants" in La Terre. The outline of the novel clearly delineates the relationship of the peasants to the earth, as Zola defines the role that the earth itself is to play: "La terre nourricière, la terre qui donne la vie, et qui la reprend, impassible.... L'homme, le paysan, n'est qu'un insecte s'agitant sur elle, peinant pour lui arracher sa vie.... Et surtout son impassibilité, son indifférence pour l'individu : Tout pour la vie qu'elle entretient." (531-532)

The insect simile and apathetic nature also combine in the sabotage of the train in *La Bête humaine*. The crime is both plotted and perpetrated in a serene natural setting by Flore, who cannot have Jacques for herself. Throughout a warm, starry night, she plots to derail or otherwise destroy the train that will carry Jacques in the engine and his mistress Séverine in the first coach. The spring day dawns fresh and pure as the rising sun spreads its rose-colored rays over "the lively gaiety of the earth" (287). Flore manipulates the train wreck in which many passengers perish or are critically hurt. "...la radieuse matinée d'avril triomphait au-dessus du champ de massacre, baignant de la pluie douce et gaie de son clair soleil les mourants et les morts." (303) And the workers who clear the debris are compared to so many insects repairing their devastated ant hill.

Nature may seem especially apathetic when man chooses to destroy himself foolishly. In *Le Docteur Pascal*, the "joy" of a summer sun infectiously imparts to the exterior of Macquart's house the appearance of "laughing with gaiety", but belies the human tragedy within (201-204). Félicité calls upon her habitually drunk uncle who reputedly has not sobered from his last drinking bout two weeks earlier. In falling asleep, he has let his lit pipe drop upon his lap. And, shortly after Félicité's arrival, he ignites before her eyes. She calmly watches the blue flames, a color distinctive to burning alcohol, dance over his skin, crackle and crack it, and then melt the alcohol-saturated fatty flesh beneath. Unable to arouse him from his comatose stupor of inebration, she leaves him to burn and rushes out of the house "into the gayful sun, into the pure air" (203). On the following day, remarkable for "the immense serenity of the sky", Dr. Pascal and Clotilde stop at Macquart's house (205). Since he does not answer, they enter. A nauseous charred stench assails their nostrils. Beneath a cloud of stagnant, sooty smoke and in front of a half-burned chair, lie a pool of grease, a little pile of ashes, and a pipe, the sole remains of the old man, unwittingly self-immolated to alcohol.

Apathetic fallacy serves then to condemn man when he massacres man in war, commits crimes of murder, destruction and self-destruction, or even wreaks injustice on his fellow man. The cheerful sunlight that beams sympathetically upon the "Fat Ones" of Les Halles, in *Le Ventre de Paris*, shines apathetically upon the lone black figure of Florent, one of the "Thin Ones". But even more importantly, apathetic fallacy rebukes ironically the honesty of the "Fat Ones". Bright sunlight often plays a major role here. Lisa Quenu, one of the latter, has informed the police of the subversive activities of Florent, her brother-in-law. Shortly before his arrest, the sun splashes "des gaîtés blondes" on the sidewalks along which he walks. As usual, the façade of Quenus' building, in which Florent occupies a room at the top, shines smugly in the sunshine. "En haut, sur la terrasse, le grenadier était tout fleuri." (310)

This Janus-faced phenomenon also appears in winter scenes where nature, while sympathetic to individuals of a privileged class, is apathetic to a destitute multitude. In *Germinal*, it is on "un jour gai de grande gelée" that the starved miners cry out for bread on their protest march across the countryside (314). As Mme Hennebeau, her daughter Cécile, and two other well-to-do ladies, return at the "limpid" close of this "beautiful winter day" spent leisurely at Marchiennes, the enraged impoverished miners approach along the same road (362). Zola had employed this stark contrastive technique very early in his career, in the short story "Les Épaules de la marquise". The heroine awakens at noon to learn from her maid that it is so bitterly cold outside that a man froze to death during the night. The marchioness claps her hands and exclaims happily that she can ice-skate that afternoon. The snow-brightened "cheerful" light floods into her bedroom; the "pretty" gray sky reminds her of the ballroom gown she wore the evening before (CN 322).

Sometimes a character himself recognizes the impassivity of nature. Shortly before his death in a duel, Philippe, of *Les Mystères de Marseille*, reflects on the irony of fate that has led him back to the same pine-enclosed clearing where he first fell in love with Blanche. "Le décor était le même, le vaste ciel s'étentait avec la même limpidité, la campagne étalait des horizons aussi doux et aussi paisibles." (248) In *Le Vœu d'une morte*, Daniel's sorrow deepens as he observes that the "joy of the day" and the sunny Parisian scene mirror in no manner whatsoever his personal grief over the death of his benefactress (32). Most of the followers in the funeral cortege quickly forget the solemnity of the occasion, smile, begin to converse, and then slacken their pace in the warm sunshine of the "cheerful" spring morning (34). And Zola himself seems to accuse the sun of indifference to Flaubert's death on the day of the funeral. Leaving the grim spectacle of Flaubert's too large casket reclining at an awkward angle in its burial place, Zola and Daudet accompany Goncourt into the town which seems completely oblivious of the loss of its most prominent citizen. Equally unaware or indifferent, the afternoon sun "allumait la Seine dont les reflets dansaient sur les façades blanches des restaurants" (RN 145).

Nature may be apathetic toward man's death even after it seems instrumental in that death. The Chanteclair, a name ironic in context, is a river that flaunts its apathy for the hero's suicidal drowning in the short story "Pour une nuit d'amour". On balmy evenings Julien Michon plays his flute, hopefully relying upon the charm of the music to eventually attract the attention and interest of Thérèse de Marsanne. After ignoring him for an entire year, she finally beckons to him one autumn evening. She will permit him to possess her provided he first remove the body of her lover who now lies dead on her bed. Under cover of night Julien disposes of the corpse in the Chanteclair. Utterly exhausted, he pauses to look down from the bridge into the musically flowing river, laughing in its eddies. The silvery reflections of the stream glinting among the "velvety" shadows of the trees fixedly retain his gaze, "et ce coin de nature lui semblait comme une promesse de paix, de bercement sans fin, dans une jouissance discrète et cachée" (CN I 285-286). His passion for Thérèse cedes to an irresistible need for eternal sleep, and he lets himself fall into the waters, and drowns. "Et le Chanteclair reprit sa chanson dans les herbes." (CN I 287)

Earlier foreboding notes had already prophesied the fatal tragedy in the stream. When Julien heard Thérèse open her window, he looked over at her "hôtel lugubre que le crépuscule noyait d'ombre. Il avait plu le matin, les marronniers, à moitié dépouillés, exhalaient une odeur de mort." (CN I 267) This succinct description already contains the basic components that Zola manipulates to impart a sensation of prophetic doom. Integrated with obvious words of ill omen, the key imagery both alludes to water (in this instance, "drowned" and "rained") and describes actual flowing water (the Chanteclair). Water then can become a fatal stream, an irreversible course to tragedy.

3. PROPHETIC FALLACY OR THE FATAL STREAM

> C'est le bruit de ces flots, de ce vent qui murmure,
> C'est l'aspect de ces bois, c'est toute la nature
> Qui me brise le cœur, et qui me fait mourir!

> Musset

It will be recalled that, in the section entitled "The Stream of Love", slow moving, sometimes sensuous, waters provide an essential element of an ideal natural setting for lovers. But flowing waters can also become a fatal stream, or even a stream of love and a fatal stream at the same time or at different times. The relationship between love and death in flowing waters may stem from a childhood memory that Zola recalls in the third of his "Souvenirs": "Bonne rivière..., je t'aime encore comme une maîtresse enfantine. Tu nous as pris un camarade, un soir, ...et c'est peut-être cette tache de sang sur ta robe verte qui a laissé en moi des frissons de désir pour ton maigre filet d'eau. Il y a des sanglots, dans ton babil d'innocente." (CN 390) Perhaps that bloodstain gave impetus to the short story "Le Sang", a series of nightmares in which the rivulets of blood flowing from the wounds of those slaughtered on the battlefields form a continuously swelling stream of blood that eventually runs over the entire world (CN 120).

The Durance, Garonne, and Seine are literally fatal rivers for some of Zola's characters. The action of "Hiver", the fourth and final section of "Les Quatre journées de Jean Gourdon", begins on a "sinister" January morning. Through the thick cloak of a gigantic thaw, the countryside resembles a large, torn, "dirty gray rag" (CN 459). (This image of a ripped rag full of holes has its counterpart in the trees half-stripped of their leaves in "Pour une nuit d'amour", a description quoted at the conclusion of our preceding section.) The oaks with their upraised "black arms" stand like "une rangée de spectres gardant l'abîme de vapeur qui se creusait derrière eux" (CN 460). The opaque shadows of the thickening fog wall up the windows, and night falls in mid-afternoon. A hoarse howl rises and fills the dark abyss beyond, and the farm itself seems "suspended in the middle of a pit" (CN 462). The source of the ominous sound remains obscure until water begins to enter the house. As the rapidly rising waters of the Durance gradually engulf the house, Jean and his family board a makeshift raft. Sinister images are rewoven into the description for these now powerless victims of the fatal river: "Nous descendions avec une rapidité effrayante. De grands nuages, des haillons sales et troués traînaient dans le ciel; puis, lorsque la lune se cachait, une obscurité lugubre tombait. Alors nous roulions dans le chaos." (CN 468)

In the short story "L'Inondation", for which "Hiver" may be the model, the stress shifts from a prophetic to an apathetic nature. Ironically, the Garonne, a perennial benefactor throughout Louis Roubieu's long life, ultimately destroys the old man's past, present and future. It floods his land, drowns the livestock, sweeps away the servant girls, and forces the family to take refuge on the roof. The premonition of disaster, drastically condensed in this later version of the tale, looms now as the family peers apprehensively into the dusk: "Une clarté louche flottait au-dessus de la nappe limoneuse. Le ciel pâle avait l'air d'un drap blanc jeté sur la terre. Au loin, des fumées traînaient. Tout se brouillait, c'était une jour épouvantée s'éteignant dans une nuit de mort." (CN I 300) Here Zola manipulates the mood of imminent doom with more sophistication and greater control. The Gothic and specific images of "Hiver" are transmuted now into vaguely sensed and less clearly visual images that dip subtly below the surface of the reader's consciousness. Shapeless masses already seem to float and swirl into a great, mist-shrouded void. Sky, earth, and water become as one through the cloth metaphors, suggestive of immense shrouds. However, with the fall of night, nature appears apathetic in the "sovereign greatness" of the nocturnal sky. But this "spectacle" with its "pure" blue starlight is less convincing (CN I 302). Louis can only look on helplessly while one member after the other of his family perishes in the flood. As night ends he hears someone laughing near him. The beautiful light of dawn discloses that it is his Marie. As she continues to laugh hysterically, he begins to laugh like her. Passively she lets herself slip into the waters, leaving the old man totally alone.

The Seine, another 'fatal' river, portends and awaits Camille's murder by drowning in *Thérèse Raquin*. Premonitory signs of the imminent tragedy appear in the description of nature as Laurent slowly rows the boat, which also bears Camille and Thérèse, toward some islands in the river. "De grandes ombres tombaient des arbres, et les eaux étaient noires sur les bords." (68) The temperature drops as the shroud of dusk descends: "L'eau et le ciel semblaient coupés dans la même étoffe blanchâtre." (68) The three characters lapse into silence as they approach the islands. Signs of life fade and slip into oblivion. Even the rich vital reds of the trees have turned somber. Somewhat similar to the scene from "L'Inondation" where the landscape dissolves into floating shrouds, "la Seine, le ciel, les îles, les coteaux n'étaient plus que des taches brunes et grises qui s'effaçaient au milieu d'un brouillard laiteux" (69).

This same river augurs Claude's suicide in *L'Œuvre*. Murky blacks and blood reds augment the tones of pathos and premonition. A large, phosphorescent red cloud hovers in the soot black winter sky. Claude stands alone at the parapet of Le Pont des Saint-Pères. The despondent artist strains anxiously to discern at least the outline or shape of the forepart of La Cité, the subject of his current and most ambitious painting. However, the deep shadows of night have swallowed all but the silhouettes of some bridges in the foreground. "Puis, au delà, tout se noyait, l'île tombait au néant, ... Une lanterne rouge, au ras du barrage de la Monnaie, jetait dans l'eau un filet de sang. Quelque chose d'énorme et de lugubre, un corps à la dérive, une péniche détachée sans doute, descendait avec lenteur au milieu des reflets, parfois entrevue et reprise aussitôt par l'ombre." (371) The somber color of blood reappears as Claude, wondering whether the island might be submerged at the bottom of the Seine, leans forward to look down into "ce fossé si large, d'une fraîcheur d'abîme", and watches the reflections of gas lamps convert the murmuring river into burning embers. "Et le gros bruit triste du courant l'attirait, il en écoutait l'appel, désespéré jusqu'à la mort." (371) However, unlike Julien in "Une Nuit d'amour", Claude resists "cette douceur de mourir" in the river, only to hang himself some hours later in front of his unfinished painting of the scene that refused to materialize for him from the bridge.

The Meuse river, in *La Débâcle*, carries omens of the French defeat by the Prussians at Sedan. A melancholy dusk "drowns" the streets of the city. "Le gros bruit de la Meuse continuait, une plainte d'infinie tristesse semblait avoir passé dans l'ombre croissante." (189) The concept of the fatal stream extends metaphorically to the description of the marching troops of the 106th regiment as they "stream" across the lonely, dismal plains of Champagne. Imagery of flowing water describes their forward march for which there is no turning back. The interminable road, down which the troops march, leads straight across the monotonous plains, disturbed only by ominous notes, such as flights of crows and windmills "agitating" their wings (77-78).

Fatal streams are not only prophetic of violent deaths and major catastrophes, but also prophesy imminent personal misfortunes and tragedies of love.

The Seine flows sluggishly to portend Rougon's second fall from power, in *Son Excellence Eugène Rougon*. Although he has tendered his resignation, Rougon is hopeful that the Emperor will refuse it. However, at the charity bazaar held in the Orangerie des Tuileries, his hopes are dashed when he recognizes a certain choker around Clorinde Delestang's neck. This necklace is a blatant declaration that she has become the Emperor's mistress and that her husband naturally will rise to power now while he, Rougon, will fall from it. He leaves in disgust. A storm brews in the sky. "En bas, la Seine, huileuse, d'un vert sale, coulait lourdement entre les quais blafards." (377) A heavy downpour detains him at home for almost an hour. When he resumes his walk up the Champs-Elysées, the fatal stream shifts to this central artery of Paris as it turns into a river of yellow mud. "Au ciel, l'orage avait laissé une queue de haillons cuivrés, toute une nuée sale, basse, d'où tombait un reste de jour mélancolique, une lumière louche de coupe-gorge." (380) The fatal stream also flows muddily for his brother Aristide, another protagonist who falls from power, in *L'Argent;* together with the streaming yellow mud, a glacial winter rain and metaphors of drowning stand out in relief to portend and punctuate the plunge from his pinnacle position in the stock market (346-356).

A muddy fatal stream flowing beneath an ominous crepuscular sky of smudged and ragged clouds, in *Le Ventre de Paris*, foreshadows Florent's arrest on the following day. Lisa has already informed the police about the subversive activities of her brother-in-law. "La nuit venait, une pluie fine ... noyait de gris les grandes Halles. Elles se détachaient en noir sur les fumées rousses du ciel, tandis que des torchons de nuages sales couraient, presque au ras des toitures, comme accrochés et déchirés à la pointe des paratonnerres. Florent était attristé par le gâchis du pavé, par ce ruissellement d'eau jaune qui semblait charrier et éteindre le crépuscule dans la boue." (286)

The narrow by-street called the Passage des Eaux, appropriately named during wet spells, serves the fatal stream concept on two successive days, in *Une Page d'amour*. It forebodes the sullying of the platonic love of Hélène Grandjean for Henri Deberle in an act of adultery and consequently, because of her absence from home, her daughter's death. As a concierge, Mère Fétu has access to the apartment of Mme Deberle's lover and volunteers to show it to Hélène. Just before reaching the building, Hélène must descend the Passage des Eaux and its rivulets of muddy, melting snow. They form a slushy stream that teems with ominous signs: "Le passage s'ouvrait sous ses pieds comme un trou noir.... A droite et à gauche, les murs se resseraient, allongés démesurément par la nuit, tandis que les branches dépouillées des arbres, au-dessus, mettaient vaguement des profils de bras gigantesques, aux mains tendues et crispées.... La boue était si épaisse, que ses bottines restaient collées sur les marches." (235-236) The next morning she sends an anonymous letter to Henri; then relenting, she hastens to warn the pair before Henri arrives to discover his wife in the arms of another man. The Passage des Eaux, now a torrent, seems to presage the sweeping away of her resistance to Henri's passionate entreaties (254). In the meantime her frail daughter, who feels abandoned at home, catches a fatal cold in the drenching rain at the open window as she peers out stubbornly for some sign of her mother in the city below. The fatal stream concept, complete with its introductory sinister imagery and the presence of a muddy Seine, voluminously expands to engulf Paris which, under the sustained assaults of the heavy downpour, "drowns", "submerges" like a "sunken" city, and finally "dissolves" from view (267-278).

Another passage, though totally waterless, appropriates characteristics typical of the other descending currents that lead fatefully to tragedy, in *La Fortune des Rougon*. The dry lane down which Silvère is led now to his execution formerly imparted to Silvère and Miette on nocturnal strolls the pleasant sensation of floating down a river (37). But this 'stream of love' for them is transformed here into a 'fatal stream' for him alone. "Le crépuscule jaune tombait comme une boue fine sur les ruines de ses chères tendresses." (337) He is one of two hostages to be shot in retaliation for the participation of the town of Plassans in the uprising against the Empire. Not only is the lane desolate, lugubrious, and cast in "muddy tints", but it also possesses "un aspect vague de torrent desséché" (336). The rust-colored remnants of daylight "die". (338) Thus, this transfigured fatal 'stream' courses like its watery counterparts through traditionally ominous autumnal or wintry dusks and nights to prophesy the imminence of personal tragedy, violent death or major catastrophe.

4. MALEVOLENT FALLACY

> Ne me laisse jamais seul avec la Nature,
> Car je la connais trop pour n'en pas avoir peur.

Vigny

Nature appears not only to forebode the doom of man, but even to loom up directly before him on occasion as a maleficent or malignant being, against which he must engage in personal combat, frequently for his own life. The apparently hostile natural phenomena which the helpless human victim battles most often are flooding waters, the sea, encroaching organic growth, or the earth itself.

Man struggles furiously but futilely with flooding rivers in two instances. The hero of "Les Quatre journées de Jean Gourdon" attributes anger and a life of its own to the deluging Durance. Jean has evacuated his family onto a makeshift raft that he and his son try in vain to direct with poles toward the shore. But immediately they find themselves in close combat "avec la rivière comme avec un être vivant, cherchant à la vaincre, à la blesser, à la tuer. Elle nous serrait entre ses bras de géant, et nos perches devenaient, dans nos mains, des armes que nous lui enfoncions en pleine poitrine avec rage. Elle rugissait, elle nous jetait sa bave au visage, elle se tordait sous nos coups." (CN 467) In "L'Inondation", Louis Roubieu and the younger men of the family ward off with poles the floating debris which the fast current of the swollen Garonne smashes like ramrods against the rooftop, the last refuge for the family. "Peu à peu, ils perdaient la tête, jurant, tapant, insultant l'eau. Gaspard la sabrait, comme s'il se fût pris corps à corps avec elle, la trouait de coups de pointe ainsi qu'une poitrine. Et l'eau gardait sa tranquille obsination, sans une blessure, invincible.... Le combat était impossible." (CN I 307-308) [Like the heroes of these two short stories who battle and swear at flooding rivers, other characters curse and futilely threaten the sky for its seemingly hostile attacks against them. In *L'Assommoir*, Gervaise and Coupeau's wedding party, infuriated by the persistent rain, swear and shake their fists at the clouds (73). In *L'Œuvre*, Claude menaces the sky with his fist for repeatedly sending its winds to carry off his easel and its rains to cut short his outdoor painting sessions (227). La Grande, of *La Terre*, upon seeing how a hailstorm has damaged her fruits and vegetables, crudely reviles the sky and tries to puncture it with rocks she furiously throws upward (116).]

As a child, the heroine of *Thérèse Raquin* engaged in imaginary combat with the Seine. Lying prone beside the Seine, Thérèse would dig her fingers, cat-like, into the earth, and imagine herself fighting the river: "...elle regardait avec défi la rivière qui grondait, elle s'imaginait que l'eau allait se jeter sur elle et l'attaquer; alors elle se roidissait, elle se préparait à la défense, elle se questionnait avec colère pour savoir comment elle pourrait vaincre les flots." (13)

To conquer the destructive action of the ocean waves is a recurrent challenge in *La Joie de vivre*, a novel that primarily pits man against the sea. Even on Pauline Quenu's first evening in her new home, the roaring sea rages with deafening din. A chaotic wall of shadows temporarily blocks out the outer view. The sound of the crashing breakers, like an artillery barrage, shakes the house. The small fishing village of Bonneville below and the coastal rocks seem "drowned" beneath the "inky waves" (30). Lazare Chanteau nurtures a project to vanquish the continuous efforts of the sea to undermine the village. With the construction of an immense breakwater, he hopes to stop the corroding attacks upon the cliffs where the villagers stubbornly persist in dwelling. With the thought that this philanthropic action might make Lazare famous, "toute la maison ne rêvait plus que d'humilier la mer, de l'enchaîner au pied de la terrasse dans une obéissance de chien battu" (112). Pauline decides to loan Lazare the necessary funds as she watches the incoming tide bombard Bonneville one night and thinks she hears with each smashing breaker, "the howling of the poor wretches eaten by the sea" (113).

The artificial breakwater is built, but eventually stormy seas destroy it.

Lazare and Pauline witness the final decisive blows of the mountainous tide crash down upon the man-made structure. The "army" of massive waves with their "big greenish backs" and "manes of foam" hurl themselves like monstrous "battering rams" (200). In the last chapter of the novel, the ocean ultimately vanquishes the village while May storms crush the remaining houses against the cliffs. "C'était fini, les grandes marées avaient achevé de balayer le village, après des siècles d'assaut, dans l'envahissement continu de la mer, qui chaque année mangeait un coin du pays." (338) Yet the fishermen remain doggedly by the sea and build their homes further up into the ravine, "en attendant que le flot les délogeât encore, après de nouveaux siècles de bataille" (339).

Encroaching grasses and underbrush metamorphose metaphorically into a sea of attacking waves that threatens to engulf and drown the human being. Section XI of "Souvenirs" describes the losing battle the old woman called La Sarcleuse has been waging for fifty years against the grasses, weeds, and wild flowers which attempt to take over the grounds of the castle at Versailles. The wildly growing vegetation menaces the crumbling castle itself. La Sarcleuse can recount the historical progress achieved by these weeds: their timidity during the reign of Charles X, their aggressiveness with the advent of Louis-Philippe, and their triumph in the Second Empire. To pull up the weeds from one end of the grounds to the other is a month-long task for the old woman. "Et, derrière elle, l'herbe repousse, victorieuse, si drue, si implacable, que, lorsqu'elle recommence son éternelle besogne, elle retrouve les mêmes herbes poussées de nouveau, les mêmes coins de cimetière envahis par les fleurs grasses." (CN 412) Zola imagines her as the ghost of some marchioness, sentimentally attached to the ruins, who has assigned herself this "besogne vaine, sentant bien que si elle s'arrêtait un jour, le flot des herbes déborderait et la noierait elle-même" (CN 413). Zola envisions the eventual collapse of the castle and the complete victory of the weeds, the thistles, and the thick, twisting underbrush on the day when the old woman's fingers shall finally stiffen. "Et la Sarcleuse se perdra dans les fourrés, écartant des poignées de tiges plus hautes qu'elle, se frayant un passage au milieu de brins de chiendent grands comme de jeunes bouleaux, luttant encore, jusqu'au jour où ces brins la lieront de toutes parts, la prendront aux membres, à la taille, à la gorge, pour la jeter morte à cette mer qui la roulera dans le flot toujours montant des verdures." (CN 413)

This last image reappears in *La Faute de l'abbé Mouret*, where the autumnal scene chills Serge upon his return to the Paradou. The grasses in the prairies are shoulder-high and are like "autant de bras minces qui cherchaient à le lier aux membres, pour le rouler et le noyer au fond de cette mer verte, interminable" (373). The invasive force of organic growth is a recurrent image in the novel. Jeanbernat, guardian of the Paradou, confesses to Abbé Mouret and Dr. Pascal that he has not ventured into the park proper for the past twelve years. He finds the Paradou too large and too dark, its vegetation too thickly overgrown, and its nearness overwhelming. "Et je me suis barricadé, pour que le parc n'entrât pas." (58) Even the plants in the flower-bed of the Paradou, untended for the past century, increase in size each year, propagate themselves in complete abandon, and invade every available spot. Creeping plants pull down the marble statues, and shrubs uproot the tiles of the terraces. The encroaching vegetation seems to willfully undo the former efforts of man to mold nature to his will (180).

A trespassing nature enters hostilely and rends asunder the church in which the hallucinating priest fulfills his duties. The actual invasion begins rather unobtrusively early in the novel as the priest celebrates Mass to an absent congregation. The sun spreads itself throughout the church, the service tree pokes its budding branches through the broken panes of a window, bushes begin to uproot the steps, and the incursion of grasses and herbs is imminent (18, 20, 22, 28). The hallucinatory upheaval of the church takes place after the idyllic interlude in the Paradou. Albine comes into the church to enticingly entreat the priest to return with her to the park, but he withstands the temptation and sends her away. His flesh weakens when his thoughts dwell increasingly on Albine and the happy times spent with her in the Paradou. An overpowering hallucination begins to engulf his mind. The flaming red rays of the setting sun seem to burn the walls and ceiling. Sudden night blackens the church but activates his auditory sensitivity. A growing murmur from the valley reaches the ears of the priest who feels himself once again a man of flesh with physical needs. The hills quake as rocks and stones roll forward of their own momentum and cultivated fields flow forward. The entire valley moves like an attacking army toward the church: "...les souches des vignes rampaient comme de grands insectes; les blés maigres, les herbes séchées, faisaient des bataillons armés de hautes lances; les arbres s'échevelaient à courir, étiraient leurs membres, pareils à des lutteurs qui s'apprêtent au combat; les feuilles tombées marchaient, la poussière des routes marchait." (355) Livestock and other domestic animals join in the assault. Herbs, grasses, and mosses undermine the construction of the edifice by slipping their "fingers" and roots around the bricks and tearing out the masonry. The dried grasses slide under the door to rip up the flooring-tiles. "C'était l'émeute victorieuse, la nature révolutionnaire dressant des barricades avec des autels renversés, démolissant l'église qui jetait trop d'ombre depuis des siècles." (357) The service tree deals the mortal blow when, after its lunge down into the midst of the nave, it swells its trunk and furiously multiplies its branches in order to tear apart the remains of the walls and roof and to explode the rest into dust (357). The deluded priest applauds the total victory of nature, all of its phenomena and life united in league, over the church, for now God can no longer stop him from rejoining Albine in the Paradou.

In *Germinal* the earth eventually avenges itself upon the miners who have cut into its artery of coal. The miners trapped in the mine reason that "c'était la terre qui se vengeait, qui lâchait ainsi le sang de la veine, parce qu'on lui avait tranché une artère" (514). The avenger of the earth appears to Catherine in the superstitious figure of the *Homme noir* who strangles bad little girls. She points out this imagined black figure to Etienne and explains: "La terre a lâché tout le sang de la veine, pour se venger de ce qu'on lui a coupé une artère." (530)

The struggle between man and nature is eternal on the plains of Beauce in *La Terre*. Viewed from a distance, the peasants who sow the seed seem like so many busy "black ants" with "cet entêtement d'insectes en lutte avec l'immensité au sol, victorieux à la fin de l'étendue et de la vie" (20). Zola illustrates vividly this concept of the real and final victory of the earth over the peasants in a harvest scene. The peasants, seen from afar, appear victorious: "Les insectes grêles, noyés dans ce travail géant, en sortaient victorieux." (241) However, a close-up of an individual harvester belies the distant perspective. Under the searing August sun the thirty-five year old Palmyre, so exhausted by the constant years of physical labor that she appears to be sixty, cries out painfully and falls to the ground, "la face au ciel, les bras en croix, comme crucifiée sur cette terre, qui l'avait usé [*sic:* usée] si vite à son dur labeur, et qui la tuait" (251). She dies in the midst of the rich harvest. The earth is victorious.

5. BENEVOLENT FALLACY AND THE CHAIN OF BEING

> Le ciel s'illuminait d'un sourire divin.
>
> Hugo

Man was seen in the preceding section to regard nature as hostile. But malevolence may mask ultimate benevolence. Nature wears many dis-

guises, sometimes one over the other. Some men will discover malevolence in nature to be a mask disguising impassivity which, perceived by the
more philosophical and mystic, may be in itself another mask that conceals benevolence. In his outline for *La Terre*, Zola stipulates that the
main characteristic of the earth will be its "indifférence pour l'individu:
tout pour la vie qu'elle entretient. La naissance, la mort, ce sont des états,
des mots; elle ne fait que de la vie, allant à un but inconnu. Les insectes
qui vivent d'elle, qu'elle laisse faire pour le grand but." (531-532).

In essence, then, the earth and nature in general are not malevolent but,
rather, indifferent to the human condition. They evolve and propel themselves forward to their own goal, unknown by man, this unenlightened
participant. In the same outline, Zola goes on to assert that the seemingly
impassive earth is actually both "beautiful" and "good". These qualities
will stand in sharp contrast with the "meanness" of the possessive
peasant. The author plots that Jean Macquart, not born a peasant, shall
return from the war to seek the "calmness" of the earth. However, he
shall not find peace there because of his constant clashes with "l'homme
mauvais sur la terre grande et bonne. Cela me donne absolument ce fait
que je cherchais, la vilenie de l'homme sur la terre belle." (532) Contrary
to the indigenous peasants, Jean will remain sensitive to the beauty of
the earth; and at the end of the novel, he will become aware of "la moisson future, le secret de la terre qui fait toujours de la vie avec la mort,
allant à son but inconnu" (533).

In his repeated insistence upon the "unknown goal" of the earth, Zola
restates the question, and renews the concept of the "great chain of
being".[5] As a matter of fact, Zola was planning in 1860 to compose an
epic poem entitled "La Chaîne des Etres".[6] Zola's concept of the chain of
being links with the thought and attitude of some eighteenth-century
philosophers. In an essay on geology and history, Zola states that the
universe was not created for man; rather, "nous avons été créés à l'usage
du grand Tout, de l'œuvre qui s'élabore depuis le commencement des
temps" (MH 107). Our lives serve to "avancer d'un pas la création vers
le but inconnu. Il y a je ne sais quelle grandeur, quelle paix suprême,

---

[5] For the historical evolution of this concept, see Arthur O. Lovejoy, *The Great Chain
of Being; A Study of the History of an Idea* (Cambridge, Mass.: Harvard Univ. Press,
1936).
[6] F. W. J. Hemmings, in *Émile Zola* (Oxford: Clarendon Press, 1953), pp. 37-38, finds
that the concept of its proposed three cantos tracing the past, present, and future of
man in "the unbroken chain of evolution" strikingly sets the pattern for Zola's three
series of novels: *Les Rougon-Macquart* in the past, *Les Trois villes* in the present, and
Les Quatre Évangiles in the future.

quelle joie profonde, dans cette idée que Dieu travaille en nous, que nous préparons la terre et l'être de demain, que nous sommes un enfantement et qu'au dernier jour nous assisterons, avec l'univers entier, à l'achèvement de l'œuvre." (MH 107)

Thus, the material cosmos is endowed with a perpetually self-renewing vital process that integrally involves all of its parts, all forms of life. The eighteenth-century theme of the perfectibility of man intertwines with the concept of an ongoing creative dual evolution of nature and man: "La création continue, l'œuvre marche, grandit. Le labeur des mondes est éternel. Nous sentons la terre en enfantement tressaillir sous nos pieds, nous sentons la matière s'épurer en nous. Il y a encore de nouvelles contrées dans le sein de notre globe, et il y a encore dans notre être, dans nos vagues aspirations et nos désirs d'infini, de nouveaux êtres plus purs et plus parfaits." (MH 108)

When man ascribes beneficent qualities to nature, an appeal to the senses generally prompts a psychological interpretation of the universe, often followed by a philosophical view of it. The eternal cycle, of which birth, life, and death are simple 'states' of being or merely 'words', embodies the promise of rebirth. This philosophical attitude of nature and man recreating life from the raw materials of their life and death offers an optimistic and new, though ancient in Eastern thought, dimension to human life and death for some of Zola's characters.

As death approaches, Lazare, in "Les Quatre journées de Jean Gourdon", and the autumnal landscape fade together in the sunset hour: "Il s'éteignait lentement, comme ces lueurs légères qui pâlissaient sur les hautes branches." (CN 459) But having lived long enough to see a child born to Jean and Babet, Lazare dies happily and without regret. "Le crépuscule tombait, les adieux de l'oncle Lazare nous laissaient confiants, ainsi que les adieux du soleil qui meurt le soir pour renaître le matin." (CN 459) It is in the first section of the short story that Lazare expounds his philosophy of the true intent of nature. The scene is reminiscent, both in setting and situation, of Rousseau's *Profession de foi du vicaire savoyard*. Lazare, himself a parish priest, leads the young hero along a wide lane of enormous oaks, which form a high arch above them, to a natural terrace overlooking the Durance river valley, bathed in the bright golden sunshine of early morning. With a sweeping gesture that encompasses the "joyful" landscape before them, Lazare tells Jean to look at "les premiers sourires de la jeune saison" (CN 432). The priest infers that perhaps the youth egoistically considers these natural environs to center about him: "...la grande vallée te semble un lieu de délices: la rivière est là pour te donner sa fraîcheur, les arbres pour te prêter leur ombre, la campagne entière pour te parler de tendresse, le ciel lui-même pour embraser ces horizons que tu interroges avec espérance et désir." (CN 433) Lazare then divulges what he, as an old man, now sees as the real significance behind the "charms" of spring. He loves the river and all of nature during this season because they work together to produce the fruits of summer and autumn. Pointing to a flower at their feet, Lazare contrasts Jean's and his own manner of looking upon it, an appraisal that he extends to the entire panorama: "...elle est un parfum pour toi; pour moi elle est un travail, elle accomplit sa tâche en produisant sa part de vie, une petite graine noire qui travaillera à son tour, le printemps prochain. Et, maintenant interroge le vaste horizon. Toute cette joie n'est qu'un enfantement. Si la campagne sourit, c'est qu'elle recommence l'éternelle besogne. L'entends-tu à présent respirer fortement, active et pressée?" (CN 433)

Shortly before Lazare's death, the pair scan the valley again from the same vantage point. In this section entitled "Automne", serenity characterizes the panoramic scene while winter hints of its arrival. The old priest reminds Jean of his "sermon" of more than twenty years ago when Jean was in the spring of his life. Lazare points out that Jean has now reached that season of his life when he harvests what he has sown. He continues: "L'homme, mon enfant, a été créé à l'image de la terre. Et, comme la mère commune, nous sommes éternels: les feuilles vertes renaissent chaque année des feuilles sèches; moi, je renais en toi, et toi, tu renaîtras dans tes enfants. Je te dis cela pour que la vieillesse ne t'effraye pas, pour que tu saches mourir en paix, comme meurt cette verdure, qui repoussera de ses propres germes au printemps prochain." (CN 451)

In death resides the seed of life. The short story concludes as Jean, in the 'winter' of his life, feels spring "quiver" inside him. He has lost his family, except for one daughter, and all worldly possessions to a flood. A makeshift raft keeps the two survivors afloat. Jean recalls Lazare's lesson that one never dies, and he finds consolation in the following thought: "J'ai eu les quatre saisons, et voilà que je reviens au printemps, voilà que ma chère Marie recommence les éternelles joies et les éternelles douleurs." (CN 469)

Death blossoms into new life. In the cyclical processes of nature renewed life springs forth from life, for degeneration is but a stage in regeneration. The earth which receives all dead organisms rectifies their death. Zola illustrates this time and time again with vivid imagery in cemetery settings.

For example, in "Comment on meurt", one of the "Souvenirs", the dead contribute their blood to the color of the red poppies, while the roots of rose bushes descend into the coffins to extract

... la pâleur des poitrines virginales, l'éclat sanglant des cœurs meurtris. Cette rose blanche, c'est la floraison d'une enfant morte à seize ans; cette rose rouge, c'est la dernière goutte de sang d'un homme tombé dans la lutte.
O fleurs éclatantes, fleurs vivantes, où il y a un peu de nos morts. (CN 395)

The cemetery with its high grass, its patch of red poppies, the wafting odor of new-mown hay, the bees buzzing in the sun, and the small lizards basking in the heat, is "un coin de la vie universelle, où l'âme des morts passe dans le tronc des arbres, où il n'y a plus qu'un vaste baiser de ce qui était hier et de ce qui sera demain" (CN 396). Each Sunday in May, Mathurine plucks a rose from the bush she planted on the grave of her betrothed. He seems to smile up at her from this rose, now tucked into her fichu (CN 396).

Zola himself experiences the sensation in the Père-Lachaise cemetery that the dead are only sleeping. The warm gusts of spring air are like "women's caressing breaths", while from below there seems to emanate the gentle breathing of a child in deep sleep (CN 397). Zola notices that the willow, planted in front of the grave of Musset in deference to the latter's wish (as expressed in the opening and closing stanzas of the poet's "Lucie"), is now languishing, and he muses: "Peut-être ses racines vont-elles boire, dans le cœur du mort, toutes les amertumes d'une vie gaspil-lée." (CN 397-398) Similarly, the bad character of some buried dead flares up once again in the form of persistent weeds that threaten to take over the castle grounds at Versailles, in another one of the "Souvenirs": "...une goutte de sang est peut-être tombée là, une âme mauvaise y doit être enterrée, jetant à jamais hors de terre les pointes rousses de ses char-dons. Dans ce cimetière de la royauté, les morts ont des floraisons étranges." (CN 412)

In the transition from human to plant life, death is circumvented exceptionally in the short story "La Fée amoureuse". Through her power of magic, the fairy changes Odette and Loïs into beautiful marjoram stalks, an act that permits the young lovers to "eternally" exchange their perfumes (CN 110).

Death nurturing life is a recurrent theme in *La Fortune des Rougon*. "La vie ardente des herbes et des arbres eut bientôt dévoré toute la mort de l'ancien cimetière Saint-Mittre; la pourriture humaine fut mangée avide-ment par les fleurs." (14) Often on warm evenings Silvère and Miette sit together on one of the tombstones. The plants on all sides appear like the living extensions of the buried dead who now seek to recommence their love through the young couple. "Ces herbes, qui leur liaient les pieds par les nuits de feu, et qui les faisaient vaciller, c'étaient des doigts minces, effilés par la tombe, sortis de terre pour les retenir, pour les jeter aux bras l'un de l'autre. Cette odeur âcre et pénétrante qu'exhalaient les tiges brisées, c'était la senteur fécondante, le suc puissant de la vie, qu'élaborent lentement les cercueils et qui grisent de désirs les amants égarés dans la solitude des sentiers." (226)

Whereas Silvère and Miette's love has no consummation, Serge and Albine's does, in *La Faute de l'abbé Mouret*. Their sexual union, an "entry... into the eternity of life", was willed by the combined forces of all of nature in the Paradou (255). But when Serge returns there in the fall, his former sensibilities cannot be reawakened. Therefore Albine drives him away and wanders alone about the autumnal scene. She hears the plants wish each other a happy death now and rebirth in the spring. Her love idyll ended, she senses that they also wish her to join them in death now. Albine wonders whether their plans are for her to reappear in the spring as a rosebush, a willow or a birch. "Quelle plante odorante avait besoin de ses cheveux pour accroître de ses feuilles? Quelle fleur lui demandait le don de sa peau de satin, la blancheur pure de ses bras, la laque tendre de sa gorge? A quelle arbuste malade devait-elle offrir son jeune sang? Elle aurait voulu être utile aux herbes qui végétaient sur le bord des allées, se tuer là, pour qu'une verdure poussât d'elle, superbe, grasse, pleine d'oiseaux en mai et ardemment caressée du soleil." (387) This general setting reappears in a scene from *Le Docteur Pascal*, although the Paradou itself has long since disappeared. Pascal tells Clotilde that there will be grape and wheat harvests in its stead and that love, too, will spring anew there. "La vie est éternelle, elle ne fait jamais que recommencer et s'accroître." (55)

The eternal cycle moving from life into death and on into renewed and greater life suggests an ever expanding spiral, a willed thrust by the combined forces of nature toward a common goal. In effect, all of life in nature assume at times a kind of *élan vital* toward a universal soul.

While the hero of *La Confession de Claude* holds a wake over the body of a deceased friend, he wonders where her soul has gone: "Dans la grande nature, sans doute. Je faisais ce rêve que chaque âme va au grand tout, que l'humanité morte n'est qu'un souffle immense, un seul esprit. ...au delà de la vie, il y a pénétration complète, mariage de tous avec tous, amour unique et universel." (138) Thus, he entertains the transcendental idea of the individual soul emerging, only to merge then into the one universal soul. In fact, the concept materializes before his eyes as he imagines seeing, within the calm expanses of the sky, "l'âme du monde, l'être éternel fait de tous les êtres" (138).

Satire twists one concept of the universal soul, in the "Aventures du grand Sidoine et du petit Médéric". When the animal residents on Primevère's preserve fail to agree on a universal diet to replace their present one of milk, too bland for most of the species, the stronger animals devour the weaker ones. "L'école modèle avait donc eu pour résultat la plus grande unité possible, celle qui consiste à s'assimiler autrui corps et âme. Peut-être est-ce là l'unité dont l'homme a vaguement conscience, le but final, le travail mystérieux des mondes tendant à confondre tous les êtres en un seul." (CN 259)

Zola himself wishes at times to become part of the universal soul, to absorb his self into nature. In "La Rivière", one of the "Esquisses parisiennes", he rows his boat out to the river islands on some autumn mornings. After mooring the boat in a passageway between two islands, he basks in the peaceful solitude and feels "perdu comme un atome au sein de la vaste nature" (CN I 71). There man's civilization dwindles to insignificance for him. The seeming importance of the literary and political battles fades as he perceives the eternal laboring of the forces of a serene nature. His only wish then is to merge and lose himself into that nature, that "countryside which accomplishes its task without interruption and discussion!" (CN I 72) Placing complete trust in the overall scheme of "good" nature, he confesses, in his Parisian surroundings, to a frequent yearning to "s'anéantir dans un coin perdu, au bord d'une berge en fleurs, entre deux vieux troncs de saule.... Je me coucherais sur le dos, j'étendrais mes bras dans l'herbe, et je dirais à la bonne nature de me prendre et de me garder." (CN I 78).

These imagined actions are acted out by the autobiographical Pierre Sandoz, in *L'Œuvre*, and become the point of departure for a more fully developed interpretation of the universal soul. At first Sandoz treats facetiously the concept of a universal soul, but his initial tone switches gradually to one of earnest conviction. During one of his visits with Claude near Bennecourt, the two friends relax on one of the river islands. Sandoz unfurls his gigantic project to write a twenty-volume study, restricted to one historical period, of only one family, whose members will be living documents to substantiate the theory that man is determined by his heredity and environment. Then he lies back on the earth as if wishing to enter into it. An early passage in the novel equates Sandoz and Claude's boyhood flights into nature as "une absorption instinctive au sein de la bonne nature" (37), a compact equation that opens richly to fairly evident psychoanalytic interpretation. Jesting, he asks the earth to absorb him: "...toi l'éternelle, l'immortelle, où circule l'âme du monde, cette sève épandue jusque dans les pierres, et qui fait des arbres nos grands frères immobiles...! Oui, je veux me perdre en toi, c'est toi que je sens là, sous mes membres, m'étreignant et m'enflammant, c'est toi seule qui seras dans mon œuvre comme la force première, le moyen et le but, l'arche immense, où toutes les choses s'animent du souffle de tous les êtres." (176) (Through his own name, Zola is already of this earth. The Italian noun *zolla*, of which the family name may be a variant, can mean a lump of earth or, in a broader sense, the soil.) But what started as a pleasantry has evolved into a statement of belief, and he exclaims: "...est-ce bête, une âme à chacun de nous, quand il y a cette grande âme!" (176)

In 1885, a year before the publication of *L'Œuvre*, Zola defines his concept of the universal soul that permeates man and nature, in a letter to Jules Lemaître. Zola, after pointing out that his own physiological man contrasts with Lemaître's psychological being, elaborates: "Vous isolez l'homme de la nature, je ne le vois pas sans la terre d'où il sort et où il rentre. L'âme que vous enfermez dans un être, je la sens épandue partout, dans l'être et hors de l'être, dans l'animal dont il est le frère, dans la plante, dans le caillou... Moi, je soutiens que j'ai ma psychologie, celle que j'ai voulu avoir, celle de l'âme rendue à son rôle dans le vaste monde, redevenue la vie, se manifestant par tous les actes de la matière." (C 634)

Zola's philosophical animism, therefore, does not restrict itself to the belief that an individual soul inhabits each natural object and phenomenon. Rather, one soul expands universally to encompass all forms of life. That soul is the vital organizing principle of the physical universe. Philosophical animism, at times including both the concept of the individual souls attributed to all natural objects and phenomena and the concept of the single universal soul, appealed to many French romantic writers. The general doctrine was especially developed at great lengths in poetic form. But perhaps a brief prose passage from Balzac's *La Peau de chagrin* will serve as well as, if not better than, any other romantic excerpt to illustrate the romantic tradition as renewed by Zola. Raphaël, who approaches the end of his existence, finds temporary happiness in a setting where nature is both "naive and good".[7] Raphaël integrates and blends his being into all manifestations of life in nature. "Pour lui, les formes infinies de tous les règnes étaient les développements d'une même substance, les combinaisons d'un même mouvement, vaste respiration d'un être immense qui

[7] Honoré de Balzac, *La Comédie humaine*, ed. Bibliothèque de la Pléiade, Vol. IX (Dijon: Gallimard, 1961), p. 233.

agissait, pensait, marchait, grandissait, et avec lequel il voulait grandir, marcher, penser, agir."[8]

In the depths of despair, in degeneration, destruction, and death, awaits the promise of renewed hope tendered by the evolving universal soul. A same character, Jean Macquart, perceives this in the concluding scene of two separate novels. In *La Terre*, he stands alone in a cemetery, looking down at the freshly-covered graves of his wife and old Fouan. As he sadly reflects on their murders and the other violent events that took place during the time he spent with his co-tillers of the soil, Jean reminds himself that the earth, *la nourrice*, will always be there. "La terre n'entre pas dans nos querelles d'insectes rageurs, elle ne s'occupe pas plus de nous que des fourmis, la grande travailleuse, éternellement à sa besogne." (516) He reasons that violence in both nature and man may be necessary links in the universal chain of being: "De même que la gelée qui brûle les moissons, la grêle qui les hache, la foudre qui les verse, sont nécessaires peut-être, il est possible qu'il faille du sang et des larmes pour que le monde marche. Qu'est-ce que notre malheur pèse, dans la grande mécanique des étoiles et du soleil...? Et la terre seule demeure l'immortelle, la mère d'où nous sortons et où nous retournons, elle qu'on aime jusqu'au crime, qui refait continuellement de la vie pour son but ignoré, même avec nos abominations et nos misères." (516)

And in the last scene of *La Débâcle*, Jean watches Paris burn in the setting sun. Marriage with Henriette Levasseur is now out of the question since he unwittingly killed her twin brother in the civil strife of the Commune. Thus the two beings whom he cherished most are lost to him forever, and France itself is in agony. Yet, in the sunset, Jean sees a metaphorical fresh dawn for nature and for man. "C'était le rajeunissement certain de l'éternelle nature, de l'éternelle humanité, le renouveau promis à qui espère et travaille, l'arbre qui jette une nouvelle tige puissante, quand on a coupé la branche pourrie, dont la sève empoisonnée jaunissait les feuilles." (586)[9] He exchanges a simple farewell with Henriette and

---

[8] *La Comédie humaine*, Vol. IX, p. 237.

[9] Guy Robert, in *La Terre d'Émile Zola, Étude historique et critique* (Paris: Les Belles Lettres, 1954), p. 473, demonstrates how this concept, as it appears in its variations in *La Terre* and Zola's outline for the novel, is the primary key for understanding Zola's naturalism: "... les hommes ne souilleront pas la terre; leur labeur et le don qu'ils lui font d'eux-mêmes reçoivent d'elle au contraire leur grandeur. Rien n'est maudit; et c'est là peut-être la leçon la plus profonde du Naturalisme de Zola: les plus viles réalités sont requises par l'œuvre de vie. Des fermentations et des pourritures sortent les moissons nouvelles."

walks into the future, prepared to work toward the reconstruction of a new France.

Thus, pathetic fallacy imbues even the universal soul and regenerative myths, concepts renewed by Zola. Through sympathetic and empathetic fallacy, nature reflects and augments in its magnifying mirror, the joy and misery of man. Through apathetic fallacy, an impassive nature employs irony to condemn evil or remind man of his insignificance upon this earth. Through prophetic fallacy, nature forebodes, usually in the dramatic guise of a "fatal stream", man's imminent tragedy. Through malevolent fallacy, a hostile nature avenges itself of man's attempts to suppress or exploit it. And through benevolent fallacy, 'good' nature, a multifaceted but single-minded organism, evolves continuously as it strives for perfection. Nature embraces and involves man, impelling him toward the same goal, and therein lies his hope, too. Man is swept up into the universal soul, and his death is recycled into renewed life. Death is merely a rite of passage in the evolutionary processes of the universe. Death and destruction are transitory, not final. Transmuted, they germinate into regeneration and reconstruction, the optimistic note that sounds at the end of such generally pessimistic novels as *Germinal, L'Argent*, and *La Débâcle*. Similarly, *Le Docteur Pascal*, the novel concluding the greater twenty-volume novel of *Les Rougon-Macquart*, resounds expansively of Zola's constant and ultimate optimism in the life forces of the universe, an optimism that transcends the passing misery in human events. It is the lesson that Dr. Pascal taught and bequeathed to his widowed Clotilde. In the final pages of the novel and of the series, his message inspires her with renewed hope: "La foi en la vie que le maître avait enracinée en elle, la tenait brave, debout, inébranlable. Qu'importaient les misères, les souffrances, les abominations! la santé était dans l'universel travail, dans la puissance qui féconde et qui enfante." (342) Herein lies the point of departure for, and central to, the author's final works.

Repeatedly Zola counsels man to place his faith and confidence in work, in life, and in nature. And it is precisely this multifaceted faith that leads Zola to reassure his readers that, though the naturalists are determinists, they are neither fatalistic nor pessimistic about the future: "...du moment où nous pouvons agir, et où nous agissons sur le déterminisme des phénomènes, en modifiant les milieux par exemple, nous ne sommes pas des fatalistes." (RE 32)

VII

THE "SCREEN"

> ... notre âme saisie
> Se perd dans la nature et dans la poésie.
>
> Hugo

Zola adorns and distorts nature. In using pathetic fallacy, he endows nature with something that it does not possess: the traits, feelings, and emotions of man. Nature mirrors the soul of man and, when necessary, will unfurl its infinite spaces to allow for the ample expansion of that soul. As in the romantic tradition, nature is both a sounding board and a springboard for the ego. Not only does Zola make nature sentient, but he also personifies it with attributes of human characteristics. Thus, through pathetic fallacy and poetic anthropomorphism, Zola recreates nature in the shimmering image of man himself. Nature is divested of its true externality. Its real identity is diffused as through a changeable screen.

Already in 1864 Zola considers the concept of such a screen. In a letter to Valabrègue he discusses the various 'Screens' through which the classical, romantic, and realistic writers observe nature. The classics' white, rather opaque Screen excludes color and abstracts the forms of slightly undulating lines. The romantics' Screen, tinted in the seven colors of the rainbow, is translucent in spots, transparent in others. Large areas of light and dark dramatize the shapes and images. Forms are distorted, lines broken and agitated, colors resplendent. Lively movement intensifies reality. The realists' Screen resembles a windowpane which, although supposedly clear and transparent, is clouded by a fine, gray dust: "Tout objet, en passant par ce milieu, y perd de son éclat, où plutôt, s'y noircit légèrement.... La vie s'y étale matérielle et un peu pesante." (C 255) Nevertheless, its images are the most faithful possible. Zola, who professes to admire the latter Screen, personally prefers one that transforms images into personal works of art embracing total reality: "Tout en comprenant l'Écran qui arrondit et développe les lignes, qui éteint les couleurs et celui qui avive les couleurs, qui brise les lignes, je préfère l'Écran qui, serrant de plus près la réalité, se contente de mentir juste assez pour me faire sentir un homme dans une image de la création." (C 256)

Similarly, Zola, the art critic, seeks foremost within a work of art the presence of its creator, the man. Zola finds him, for example, in Manet's "Déjeuner sur l'herbe",[1] in the paintings of Delacroix (DL 204-205), and in Michelangelo's sculptures. (MH 176) In a true work of art, the personality of the artist must never be subordinated to the objective reality of the subject matter, not even in those canvases which Zola 'applauds' for being at least realistic. In fact, for the "Salon de 1868" in which Zola lauds the depicted objectivity of nature combined with the individuality of the artist in works of Pissarro, Jongkind, and Corot, he finds that "la personnalité féconde le vrai".[2] To specify his general admiration of "the soul of nature which speaks to" the spectator from Daubigny's landscapes for the "Exposition Universelle, 1878", Zola singles out the painting "Lever de la lune, à Auvers (Seine-et-Oise)" to praise, in addition to the equally indispensable element of subjectivity, its realistic style, a far departure from "le style classique, tourné vers un idéal surnaturel, où ne se mêle rien de personnel et où la rhétorique étouffe la vie".[3] As early as the "Salon de 1866", the critic insists that "une œuvre d'art n'est jamais que la combinaison d'un homme, élément variable, et de la nature, élément fixe."[4] After requiring that the artist be not only subjective but also "powerful", Zola arrives at a definition of a work of art, a definition that he underscores: "*Une œuvre d'art est un coin de la création vu à travers un tempérament.*"[5]

As a matter of fact, the individual temperament of a writer colors his perception of the world and the objects within it. Consequently, he recreates the world in his own image. Zola considers "chaque écrivain comme un créateur qui tente, après Dieu, la création d'une terre nouvelle" (MH 141). Moreover, each writer necessarily perceives and synthesizes the world differently; "il retranche, il ajoute, il modifie, et, en somme, le monde qu'il nous donne est un monde de son invention. C'est ainsi qu'il existe, en littérature, autant d'univers différents qu'il y a d'écrivains; chaque auteur a ses personnages qui vivent d'une vie particulière, sa

---

[1] F. W. J. Hemmings and R. J. Niess, eds., *Émile Zola: Salons* (Paris: Minard, 1959), p. 96.
[2] Hemmings and Niess, p. 136.
[3] Hemmings and Niess, p. 203.
[4] Hemmings and Niess, p. 61.
[5] Hemmings and Niess, p. 73.

nature dont les paysages se déroulent sous des cieux étrangers." (MH 141)

Fifteen years later, in 1881, the critic gives even greater significance to the creative act than to the recording of objective reality. Reaffirming that "la réalité seule ne me séduit pas", Zola now clearly tolerates and even praises to some degree, provided they spring into life, those 'false' realities created by the more imaginative geniuses in writing and painting. His critical judgments here take into account "ce que l'homme ajoute à la nature, pour la créer à nouveau, d'après des lois d'optique personnelles" (DL 204-205). This is a far departure from his somewhat acquiescent acceptance of Sainte-Beuve's criticism in 1868 of *Thérèse Raquin*, particularly against Zola's eerie description of the Passage du Pont-Neuf which "n'a pas toute cette noirceur profonde et ces teintes à la Rembrandt que vous lui prêtez" (DL 226). Although conceding that Saint-Beuve is right in his plea for "average truth", yet the novelist finds it humanly natural to employ pathetic fallacy in description: "...les lieux ont simplement la tristesse ou la gaîté que nous y mettons; on passe en frissonnant devant la maison où vient de se commettre un assassinat, et qui la veille semblait banale." (DL 226) While formulating his esthetics for the novel, Zola states that when the novelist does not display both "le sens du réel et l'expression personnelle, ...autant vaudrait-il vendre de la chandelle que de se mêler d'écrire des romans" (RE 175).

When nature enters into Zola's works, one senses repeatedly the double presence of the author's temperament and the natural phenomena themselves. The latter often agitate in undefined masses and shapes, as in some of Chatcaubriand's descriptive passages. The tumultuous and passionate life which Zola ascribes to nature frequently exceeds that depicted by the romantics themselves. Victor Hugo, whose poetry Zola the youth recited in the midst of nature, and whom Zola the critic later repudiated for grossly exaggerating nature, often and ironically appears to be the prime literary father for Zola the descriptive writer of nature. In fact, the disciple fervidly vies with the master in romantic depictions of a highly animated and, at times, animistic nature. In this particular respect, Zola, as he visualizes nature, is more a late-born literary progeny of the romantics than a member of the second generation of the realists. Actually, in many respects, romanticism and realism come into confluence in Zola's naturalism.[6] Toward the end of the century Zola appears to recognize more

---

[6] Henri Barbusse in *Zola* (Paris: Gallimard, 1932), p. 80, after demonstrating that romanticism itself is a realism, shows how two movements merge and produce a new one: "Le romantisme, entre autres hardiesses, avait rattaché le lyrisme au 'Laid', mais au Laid pompeux, extravagant et ornemental, et qui reste entiché d'une noblesse de

than ever before the allegiance he owes to romanticism, even as he contrasts the latter with naturalism: "Mon credo est que le naturalism, j'entends le retour à la nature, l'esprit scientifique porté dans toutes nos
connaissances, est l'agent même du XIXe siècle. Et j'ajoute que le
romantisme, la première période, affolée et lyrique, doit nécessairement
conduire au naturalisme, la seconde période, nette et positive. Ce n'est
qu'une question d'ordre: un Etat solide doit sortir de toute insurrection,
sous peine d'effondrement final." (UC 106-107)

Zola is unlike Guy de Maupassant to whom Flaubert, the realist,
assigned the lesson of patiently and studiously observing a single object
until he discovered the peculiarities that distinguish it from all others of
its kind: "La moindre chose contient un peu d'inconnu. Trouvons-le.
Pour décrire un feu qui flambe et un arbre dans une plaine, demeurons en
face de ce feu et de cet arbre jusqu'à ce qu'ils ne ressemblent plus, pour
nous, à aucun autre arbre et aucun autre feu."[7]

Balzac, too, depicts the particularities that distinguish individual objects. His minutely detailed descriptions of milieus serve essentially to
open a panorama onto the basic character and personality of each of his
'comedians'. In his foreword to La Comédie humaine, Balzac states:
"L'animal est un principe qui prend sa forme extérieure, ou, pour parler
plus exactement, les différences de sa forme, dans les milieux où il est
appelé à se développer. Les Espèces Zoologiques résultent de ces différences."[8] He extends this concept of a determinist milieu to include the
various types of man in society, even though the objects in themselves
often seem possessed with a life of their own.

But, in contrast to Balzac's colorful selection of vivid objects to portray
man, and to Flaubert's precise depiction of the distinguishing characteristics of each object, Zola places no great significance on the true identity
of the objects themselves. Instead, he insists on how they relate to man
and extend his inner being. The externality of an object dissolves into
the sensed and emotional qualities ascribed to it by him. Rather than
being simply visible, the objects are perceived by and appeal to perhaps
all the physical senses, as well as the various levels of psychological

---

Beauté. Le naturalisme de Zola a pour caractéristique de faire entre le lyrisme et la
réalité positive, celle qui nous submerge et que nous touchons du doigt, une synthèse
qui est, dans le sens le plus pur du mot, une découverte."
[7] Guy de Maupassant, prefatory "Le Roman" of Pierre et Jean, Vol. XIX of Œuvres
complètes de Guy de Maupassant (Paris: Conard, 1909), pp. xxiii-xxiv.
[8] Honoré de Balzac, La Comédie humaine, ed. Bibliothèque de la Pléiade, Vol. I
(1956). p. 4.

awareness ranging from the conscious to the unconscious. Through these nebulous veils of perceptions, the subjective observer recreates the outer world in the image of his inner one. Sometimes the recreation for Zola and his characters takes form through poetic anthropomorphism, but most often through pathetic fallacy. The sentimental transference makes nature seem sentient, too. Zola's romantic temperament and vision transform, rather than grapple with, the objects *per se*. Sympathetic attribution permits man to evade their specific. Objective reality recedes before human sympathy and subjectivity.

As man bestows an object in the external world with his feelings and emotions, he decorates and distorts its essence; but, paradoxically, he bares more of the essence of his inner world. The passionate incrustation, while forcing the object to withdraw and alienate itself further from man, brings man closer to himself. This ornamental carapace is at times like a magnifying mirror that both reflects and intensifies man's affective being. As in romantic tradition, greater nature allows that soul to expand almost infinitely. Instead of sharp definition and details, vision cloaks recognition, as blurred outlines and suggested shapes screen and obscure the true object in itself.

Most effectively, however, Zola allows those suggestive aspects in nature, though they falsely interpret it, to reveal and define the thoughts and emotions that lie submerged below man's consciousness. In this respect, his romantic subjective imagery transcends that of the romantics as well as the realists' objective externality, in that it announces resoundingly the advent of Freudian psychology. Zola's purported return to all aspects of nature seldom probes into the nature of nature, but it plunges deeply into that of man. In a stunning paradox, Zola, who consistently champions the study of man as primarily a physiological being determined by his milieu and heredity, has actually penetrated deeper than even he may have realized into man's psyche.

> La Nature est un temple où de vivants piliers
> Laissent parfois sortir de confuses paroles;
> L'homme y passe à travers des forêts de symboles
> Qui l'observent avec des regards familiers.[9]

Through those "living pillars", man confronts reflections of his own shimmering image and, perhaps, even of the stirring emergence, from out of the thick chrysalid layers of repressions and suppressions, of his elusive psyche.

[9] Charles Baudelaire, "Correspondances", *Œuvres complètes de Baudelaire,* ed. Bibliothèque de la Pléiade (1951), p. 85.

VIII

MANKIND AND SYMBOLIC FALLACY: AN OFFSHOOT

Et je médite, obscur témoin,

Pendant que, déployant ses voiles,
L'ombre, où se mêle une rumeur,
Semble élargir jusqu'aux étoiles
Le geste auguste du semeur.

Hugo

Zola's 'scientific' study of physiological and psychological man terminates
with *Le Docteur Pascal*, the final novel of the *Rougon-Macquart* series, in
1893. During this last decade of the nineteenth century, a resurgent
interest in mysticism and the rites of Catholicism swells and threatens to
undermine not only the spirit of scientific inquiry and its ensuing societal
progress, but also the existence of naturalism in all the humanities. Zola
devotes the remaining years of his life to champion the cause of science
against religion. Assuming that a strong offense is the best strategical
defense, Zola repeatedly attacks Roman Catholicism in his next three
novels and, then, ultimately destroys it and, by extension, all ultra-
mundane directed religion in the final three novels whose action is
projected into the twentieth century. He proposes in its stead a utopian
socialism guided by reason and scientific truths.

The trilogy of *Les Trois villes* depicts the war between reason and faith
waged in the mind of Abbé Pierre Froment. In *Lourdes* the priest is
sickened by the myriad instances of the crass and commercial exploitation
of mysticism and religious superstitions. In *Rome* his faith wavers more as
he witnesses intrigues for power among the religious elite of the papal
city, this sacred citadel that remains aloof to the socio-economic problems
of the peoples of the world. In *Paris* Pierre abandons the cassock to
devote himself to replacing the asceticism of and enslavement to an ana-
chronistic Catholicism by a viable social religion based upon the truths
and discoveries of science.

The precepts of this new worldly religion are more clearly delineated and expanded into effective working doctrines by Pierre's sons in the three novels of the unfinished tetralogy, *Les Quatre Evangiles*. Mathieu of *Fécondité* praises the life forces of this world. Deeply concerned by the decreasing birth rate in France and the increasing use and misuse of birth control, Zola lyricizes the abundant procreation of man which would lead to the establishment of a creative and happy society. In this utopia that Zola presents to his reading public, man through his ingenuity and work would render fertile and productive the sterile terrains and vast wastelands of today. Luc of *Travail* sings the praises of work. He founds the "Crècherie", a utopian socialistic city for workers whose collective and cooperative, rather than competitive, efforts benefit the entire community. Man's natural instincts and passions, suppressed by Christian doctrines, are now sanctified and channeled for the good of all. Marc of *Vérité* espouses the cause of truth. A miscarriage of justice against a teaching colleague, a Jew, the Dreyfus Affair freely transposed, provides Luc with the impetus to seek out the true facts and the eventual rehabilitation of the wronged Simon. Catholicism is finally uprooted and rendered obsolete when the new generation of Cartesian thinkers, trained since the advent of improved educational methods instituted at the primary school level, accepts as truth that which is based upon scientific investigation.

Considering the contents and new direction of these novels, one may wonder what role nature can or which roles it will continue to play and to what extent. In examining these problems now, we shall observe the same thematic order as in the main body of this monograph.

The theme of 'return to nature' reemerges in only a single novel, *Fécondité*. Mathieu Froment, who works in Paris, longs for the more wholesome life and productive labor on the earth, "la mère commune de tout travail et de tout bien" (221). Once he fulfills this yearning, he next wants to multiply his progeny, already numbering five, and also his land holdings. He marks the birth of each child by clearing and plowing plots of rocky and marshy wastelands into fertile fields. Zola sings the double and repeated fecundity of earth and woman in the leitmotif that opens and closes each chapter of the Fourth Book: "Et la terre et la femme achèveraient ensemble l'œuvre de création, victorieuse des pires déchets, allant toujours à plus de vie, à plus de richesse et de force." (314) For Mathieu, these dual fruitful forces will also constitute the essence of mankind's future viable, natural religion. He envisages that the people will slough their yoke of Catholicism finally, when "la terre féconde, la femme féconde redeviendront le culte, la toute-puissance et la souveraine beauté" (683). Man's return to nature here is not patterned upon the earlier examples of real or fancied flights, generally short-lived, often the source of frustration or heartbreak. Stressing the powerful, perennial forces of the fruitfulness of the earth, this novel sounds a propagandistic clarion for an entire nation threatened by possible extinction through birth control.

The theme of 'purification and pacification' is treated briefly in a single novel, *Paris*. Pierre pleasantly surprises his brother Guillaume one sunny morning as he arrives dressed in trousers and jacket instead of the habitual priest's cassock. For Guillaume, this change of attire represents the beginning of Pierre's 'cure' from his past life, especially when he sees Pierre standing "dans le plein soleil, dans la vie que le grand vitrage laissait entrer à larges flots" (378). Another morning Marie, Guillaume's fiancée, accompanies Pierre on an outing. She remarks on his healthier appearance in the open air (386). As they bicycle together from Maisons-Laffitte toward the forest, Marie delights in the healthful aspects of cycling, in "ce retour à notre mère commune, la terre", and the "good" wind which "purifies", "calms", and "encourages" (388).

The theme of nature as a 'source of anxiety' is infrequently and only tersely noted, and then principally in *Rome*, such as when the shadows of dusk engulf certain Roman monuments and stir doubt and anxiety in Pierre's mind (64-65). No example is developed at length. Missing, too, are the instances that hint psychologically at or reveal a protagonist's repressed wish for death.

The repressed wish to return to the womb is also absent in the rare examples of the theme of nature as a 'participant in love'. Nature, as an accomplice of love, lacks the full vigor and detailed participation found in the earlier works. In *Rome*, nature only could have become an accomplice to the fulfillment of love if the young lovers had been older. Benedetta confides to Pierre that she has loved Dario since she was thirteen years old and he eighteen, that they loved each other passionately but innocently in hidden spots in the large garden of Villa Montefiori, that the scent of the ripened oranges "intoxicated" them, and that the powerful odor of the boxwoods made their hearts beat faster (235). Dario reminds her that if they had not been children then, they would have become man and wife in that garden (345). In *Paris*, immediately following the bicycling scene (just summed up in the paragraph on the theme of 'purification and pacification'), Pierre and Marie rest a while in a small sunny clearing in the woods; their friendship is deepened by a tender, mutual attraction (390-391). Although the natural setting is very pleasant, the complicity of the forest only becomes apparent later when Pierre reviews and nurtures the scene in retrospect. Alone at home, he realizes that he has fallen in love with Marie and, consequently, now looks upon that spring morning as "une matinée de fiançailles, au sein de la forêt heureuse, et la forêt complice. La nature l'avait repris, délivré de son mal, saint et fort, et l'avait donné à la femme qu'il adorait." (396) In *Fécondité*, all of nature seems not only to will the conception of the fifth child to Mathieu and Marianne, but also to share so much in its joy that the stars and earth almost swoon with Marianne at the climactic moment (101-102). However, the couple are not placed in a natural setting. Instead, the summons of nature must enter through the open bedroom window. Thus, the preceding examples demonstrate by their very paucity in number and by situations involving the immaturity of lovers, by the retrospection of apparent action, and by the somewhat removed presence of nature, a decided attenuation of the theme of nature as a 'participant in love' in these later novels.

Another difference: in these works, nature does not anthropomorphize for man.

Moreover, even the few comparisons of the earth to a woman, and man's lust for it, echo weakly from *La Terre* in sensuality and vigor; and, in their brevity, their lack of elaboration, they sound more like figures of speech now. Hearing Lepailleur curse "la terre marâtre", Mathieu of *Fécondité* counters with the remark that the earth "enfante toujours au centuple, quand on l'aime d'une solide étreinte." But Lepailleur protests that he has had his fill of "la garce" (221-222). In *Travail*, Feuillat, who farms another man's land, wishes the earth were only for those who cultivate and love it (112); professing a secret love for the earth, he longs for the day when he can love it for himself alone (162).

In fact, all the themes of man and nature reviewed thus far are attenuated greatly in both essence and proportionate frequency of examples in the post-*Rougon-Macquart* novels. In general, nature no longer interrelates, in its austere reduction of appearances, as directly, as vigorously, as intimately, or as sensually with man as before.

The only aspect that continues with relative frequency into and throughout these later novels is the remaining one, namely, pathetic fallacy. Yet, even here, certain quantitative and qualitative shifts of stress take place. One of the five varieties formerly functioning for man in nature is now totally absent; and, of the remaining four, three are represented by few examples.

Malevolent fallacy no longer threatens man.

Benevolent and prophetic fallacies are primarily limited to single novels. For benevolent fallacy, restricted to *Fécondité*, the quotations illustrating the theme of 'return to nature' in an earlier paragraph of this chapter serve equally well, if not more so, to exemplify both the 'goodness' and the constantly increasing creative forces of the earth. Prophetic fallacy is operative only in *Rome*. An outstanding and sustained illustration of this literary device unfurls throughout Chapter XI, which follows Pierre's leisurely excursion by victoria in the countryside south of Rome. The typical characteristics of prophetic fallacy are dispersed subtly in the early part of the chapter, in the descriptions of the dormant lakes of Albano and of Nemi in particular (446-448), and come into confluence during the return trip (451-452, 458, 464-466) with the added presence of the priest Santobono and his basket of poisoned figs destined for Cardinal Boccanera, but consumed instead by Dario, whose tragic end also leads to the death of his beloved Benedetta.

Apathetic fallacy appears in but two of the six novels. In *Paris* the full moon that "laissait pleuvoir à l'infini sa calme lumière de rêve" is apparently insensitive to Salvat's approaching execution, an event eagerly awaited by the amassing crowd of expectant spectators (411). Of the more numerous examples in *Lourdes*, apathetic fallacy attains its greatest graphic impact in the monstrous, nightmarish depiction of the procession of the sick and deformed pilgrims to the Grotto, a scene set in stark contrast against the beautiful nature beyond and the pure morning sun above (140-145).

Only sympathetic fallacy performs frequently in these last novels, although it wanes somewhat in the final series, *Les Quatre Evangiles*. Since this most common, obvious form of pathetic fallacy has been examined at some length in the main body of our work, it would be essentially repetitious now to cull even a sampling of its numerous typical manifestations from these later novels.

Of more significance than the dominant quantitative stress on this primary form of pathetic fallacy, is the qualitative shift of emphasis often placed on sympathetic fallacy itself. In many instances, the endowment of nature with human, at times superhuman, traits and feelings assumes manifest symbolic meaning for all mankind. Man interprets in grandiose social vision the natural phenomena before him. For example, in *Paris*, Pierre and Marie, optimistic about the future of society, watch the sun "sow" its golden rays over the city "pour la grande moisson future de justice et de vérité" (355-357). This 'natural' phenomenon recurs in even more splendor at the end of the novel (552-553), concluding with the sentence: "Paris flambait, ensemencé de lumière par le divin soleil, roulant dans sa gloire la moisson future de vérité et de justice." (553)

This last quotation represents in quintessence the vast shift of emphasis from the earlier study of man, explained in part by his interaction with nature, to solutions proposed by Zola for the betterment of mankind, solutions that consequently demand a different attitude toward nature.

In the trilogy of the three cities (a triple destructive onslaught against Catholicism) and in the later three novels (an apology of scientific truth and social reform against religious obscurantism), an active presence of nature would serve little purpose.

Zola, *un écrivain engagé* of his epoch, commits these works to the investigation of the pressing religious, ethic, and socio-economic problems of contemporary mankind. In order to present France with what he believes to be viable solutions, the author scarcely could permit his protagonists to simply flee from civilization to nature, for this would be an evasion of the moral issues that confront the community of man. The protagonist of *Fécondité* does move with his family from the city to the country, but only to found in time a large new society where the fruitfulness and vital energies of the earth serve essentially as a symbolic exemplar for mankind. In these novelized moral treatises, the apparition of natural phenomena generally edify in symbolic manner abstracted ideals for mankind.

With rare or marginal exceptions in the post-*Rougon-Macquart* series, nature has ceased to be voluptuous for man, to provide an intimate setting for him and his beloved, and to participate actively in advancing their love. Natural phenomena seldom affect man sufficiently to effect a change in his sentiments and actions. But when they do, clearly their influence is generally to a more limited extent. Nature, no longer seen to influence man, is now viewed, when seen, in symbolic light. Nature, which formerly interrelated intimately and vigorously with the body and spirit of man, eludes his grasp now as it ascends into a lofty sphere, deified for mankind. The natural phenomena transcend as exemplary symbols of inspiration for all men, summoning them to seek and find their happiness on this earth through procreation, communal work, and a constant quest for truth and justice.

Pierre, Mathieu, Marc and Luc rise above their status of mere man when each undertakes and, through lifetime efforts, fulfills one or more of these ideals for humanity. Thus the man in each protagonist absents himself in part as he, too, becomes an exemplar for mankind.

Real interaction, then, can scarcely materialize when both man and nature become, to some degree, transcendent. The interrelations of man and nature which once were so close, seemingly personal and intimate, attenuate in these later novels committed to social reforms and humanitarian ideals, until they etherealize into a rarefied relationship between mankind eternal and the radiant apotheosis of a supremely transfigured nature.

BIBLIOGRAPHY

PRIMARY SOURCES QUOTED

Zola, Émile, *Œuvres complètes*, ed. Maurice Le Blond (Paris: Bernouard, 1927-29), 50 vols.:

Short stories

Contes à Ninon, 1864.
Nouveaux Contes à Ninon, 1874.
Contes et Nouvelles, I, II.

The early novels

La Confession de Claude, 1865.
Le Vœu d'une morte, 1866.
Les Mystères de Marseille, 1867.
Thérèse Raquin, 1867.
Madeleine Férat, 1868.

Les Rougon-Macquart

La Fortune des Rougon, 1871.
La Curée, 1872.
Le Ventre de Paris, 1873.
La Conquête de Plassans, 1874.
La Faute de l'abbé Mouret, 1875.
Son Excellence Eugène Rougon, 1876.
L'Assommoir, 1877.
Une Page d'amour, 1878.
Nana, 1880.
Pot-Bouille, 1882.
Au Bonheur des dames, 1883.
La Joie de vivre, 1884.
Germinal, 1885.
L'Œuvre, 1886.
La Terre, 1887.
Le Rêve, 1888.

La Bête humaine, 1890.
L'Argent, 1891.
La Débâcle, 1892.
Le Docteur Pascal, 1893.

Les Trois villes

Lourdes, 1894.
Rome, 1896.
Paris, 1898.

Les Quatre Évangiles

Fécondité, 1899.
Travail, 1901.
Vérité, 1903.

Critical works

Mes Haines, 1866.
Le Roman expérimental, 1880.
Les Romanciers naturalistes, 1881.
Documents littéraires, 1881.
Une Campagne, 1897.

Miscellaneous

Correspondance, 1858-1902.
Mélanges

SELECTED SECONDARY SOURCES

Adam, Antoine, *Histoire de la littérature française au XVIIe siècle*, Vol. IV (Paris: Domat, 1954).

Alexis, Paul, *Émile Zola: Notes d'un ami* (Paris: Charpentier, 1882).

Bachelard, Gaston, *L'Eau et les Rêves, Essai sur l'imagination de la matière* (Paris: Corti, 1942).

L'Air et les Songes, Essai sur l'imagination du mouvement (Paris: Corti, 1943).

La Terre et les Rêveries de la Volonté (Paris: Corti, 1948).

Baillot, Alexandre, *Émile Zola; L'homme, le penseur, le critique* (Paris: Société française d'imprimerie et de librairie, 1924).

Balzac, Honoré de, "Avant-propos" of *La Comédie humaine*, ed. Bibliothèque de la Pléiade, Vol. I (Bruges: Gallimard, 1956), pp. 3-16.

La Peau de chagrin, in *La Comédie humaine*, ed. Bibliothèque de la Pléiade, Vol. IX (Dijon: Gallimard, 1961), pp. 11-249.

Barbusse, Henri, *Zola* (Paris: Gallimard, 1932).

Baudelaire, Charles, *Œuvres complètes de Baudelaire*, ed. Bibliothèque de la Pléiade (Bruges: Gallimard, 1951).

Bouvier, Bernard, *L'Œuvre de Zola* (Genève: Eggiman, 1903).

Brown, Norman O., *Life Against Death: The Psychoanalytical Meaning of History*, ed. Vintage Books (New York: Random House, 1959).

Castelnau, Jacques, *Zola* (Paris: Tallandier, 1946).

Charlier, Gustave, *Le Sentiment de la nature chez les romantiques français (1760-1830)* (Paris: Fontemoing, 1912).

Dumesnil René, *Le Réalisme et le naturalisme* (Paris: Del Duca de Gigord, 1955).

Flaubert, Gustave, *Correspondance* (Paris: Conard, 1910-12), II, 241.

Franke, Carl, *Émile Zola als Romantischer Dichter, dargestellt an seinen Beziehungen zu Victor Hugo* (Marburg a. L.: Ehrhardt Karras, 1914).

Freud, Sigmund, *The Ego and the Id*, "Standard Edition", Vol. XIX (London: Hogarth Press, 1953).

The Interpretation of Dreams, "Standard Edition", Vols. IV and V (London: Hogarth Press, 1953).

Beyond the Pleasure Principle, "Standard Edition", Vol. XVIII (London: Hogarth Press, 1955).

Goncourt, Edmond et Jules de, *Germinie Lacerteux* (Paris: Flammarion, 1921).

Grant, Elliott, *Émile Zola* (New York: Twayne, 1966).

Guillemin, Henri, *Zola légende ou vérité?* (Paris: Julliard, 1960).

Hemmings, F. W. J., *Émile Zola* (Oxford: Clarendon Press, 1953).

"The Secret Sources of *La Faute de l'abbé Mouret*", *French Studies*, XIII (1959), pp. 226-239.

Hemmings, F. W. J., and Niess, R. J., eds., *Émile Zola: Salons* (Paris: Minard, 1959).

Hugo, Victor, *Œuvres poétiques de Victor Hugo*, ed. Bibliothèque de la Pléiade, Vols. I and II (Tours: Gallimard, 1964 and 1967 resp.).

Kranowski, Nathan, *Paris dans les romans d'Émile Zola* (Paris: Presses universitaires de France, 1968).

La Fontaine, Jean de, *Fables, Contes et Nouvelles*, ed. Bibliothèque de la Pléiade (Tours: Gallimard, 1954).

Lamartine, Alphonse de, *Œuvres poétiques complètes de Lamartine*, ed. Bibliothèque de la Pléiade (Bruges: Gallimard, 1965).

Lanoux, Armand, *Bonjour, Monsieur Zola* (Paris: Amiot-Dumont, 1954).

Laporte, Antoine, *Émile Zola; L'homme & l'œuvre* (Paris: Gauterin, 1894).

Lapp, John C., *Zola before the Rougon-Macquart* (Canada: Univ. of Toronto Press, 1964).

Le Blond-Zola, Denise, *Émile Zola raconté par sa fille* (Paris: Fasquelle, 1931).

Lovejoy, Arthur O., *The Great Chain of Being; A Study of the History of an Idea* (Cambridge, Mass.: Harvard Univ. Press, 1936).

Massis, Henri, *Comment Émile Zola composait ses romans* (Paris, 1906).

Matthews, J. H., *Les Deux Zola* (Paris: Minard, 1957).

Maupassant, Guy de *Œuvres complètes de Guy de Maupassant*, Vols. XIII and XIX (Paris: Conard, 1908 and 1909 resp.).

Miles, Josephine, "Pathetic Fallacy in the Nineteenth Century", *Univ. of Calif. Publications in English* (Berkeley, 1942), Vol. XII, No. 2, pp. vi and 183-304.

Musset, Alfred de, *Poésies complètes d'Alfred de Musset*, ed. Bibliothèque de la Pléiade (Monaco: Gallimard, 1967).

Praz, Mario, *The Romantic Agony*, trans. Angus Davidson (New York: Meridian, 1956).

Proulx, Alfred C., *Aspects épiques des Rougon-Macquart de Zola* (The Hague: Mouton, 1966).

Robert, Guy, *Émile Zola; principes et caractères généraux de son œuvre* (Paris: Les Belles Lettres, 1952).

La Terre d'Émile Zola, Étude historique et critique (Paris: Les Belles Lettres, 1954).

Ruskin, John, *Modern Painters*, Vol. III, Part IV, in *The Works of John Ruskin*, eds. E. T. Cook and Alexander Wedderburn, Vol. V (London: George Allen, 1904), pp. 201-220.

Seillière, Ernest, *Émile Zola* (Paris: Grasset, 1923).

Stendhal, *La Chartreuse de Parme*, in *Romans et nouvelles de Stendhal*, ed. Bibliothèque de la Pléiade, Vol. II (Dijon: Gallimard, 1964), pp. 11-493.

Le Rouge et le Noir, in *Romans et nouvelles de Stendhal*, ed. Bibliothèque de la Pléiade, Vol. I (Tours: Gallimard, 1966), pp. 195-699.

Toynbee, Arnold J., *A Study of History* (London: Oxford Univ. Press, 1934), Vol. I, pp. 7-8.

Turnell, Martin, *The Art of French Fiction* (New York: New Directions, 1959).

Vigny, Alfred de, *Œuvres en vers*, in *Œuvres complètes d'Alfred de Vigny*, ed. Bibliothèque de la Pléiade, Vol. I (Tours: Gallimard, 1964), pp. 3-264.

Vizetelly, Ernest A., *Émile Zola, Novelist and Reformer, An Account of his Life & Work* (London: J. Lane, 1904).

Watts, Alan W., *Nature, Man, and Woman*, ed. Vintage (New York: Random House, 1970).

Wilson, Angus, *Émile Zola; An Introductory Study of his Novels* (London: Secker & Warburg, 1952).

INDEX

(The only titles included here, with the exception of *Emile Zola: Salons*, are Zola's, although other authors are listed.)